FISHING WITH HAND GRENADES

Ari Pontz

Llumina Press

The events recounted in this book are based on actual events. In most instances, names have been changed. Any similarity between fictional names and names of any person living or dead is entirely coincidental.

All letters and journal entries in this book are fictional. They have been composed by the author based on actual events.

Cover design by Corey Pontz.

© 2008 Ari Pontz

All rights reserved. No part of this publication may be reproduced or transmitted in any form or by any means electronic or mechanical, including photocopy, recording, or any information storage and retrieval system, without permission in writing from both the copyright owner and the publisher.

Requests for permission to make copies of any part of this work should be mailed to Permissions Department, Llumina Press, PO Box 772246, Coral Springs, FL 33077-2246

ISBN: 978-1-59526-910-2

Printed in the United States of America by Llumina Press

Library of Congress Control Number: 2007907468

ACKNOWLEDGMENTS

To my mother Leslie, without whose inspiration I am certain I would not have endeavored to write this book, and to my father Curt, without whose constant encouragement I am certain I would never have completed it.

And of course, my deepest thanks to "Danny," a hero—in my mind, at least.

Fishing With Hand Grenades

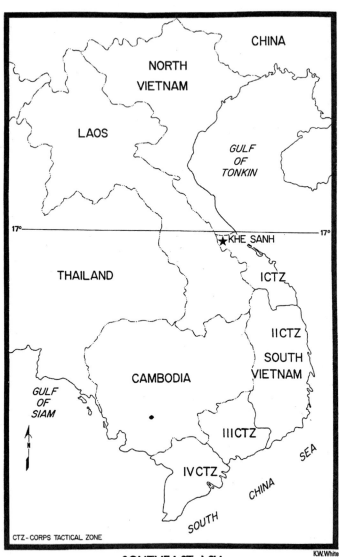

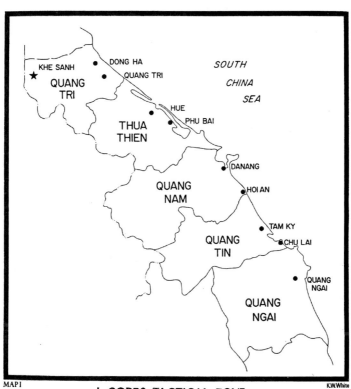

I CORPS TACTICAL ZONE

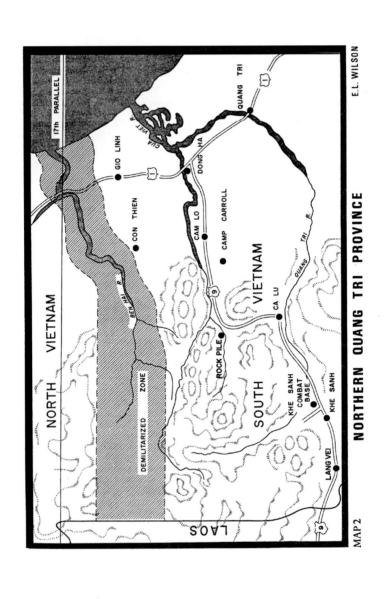

MAP 2   NORTHERN QUANG TRI PROVINCE

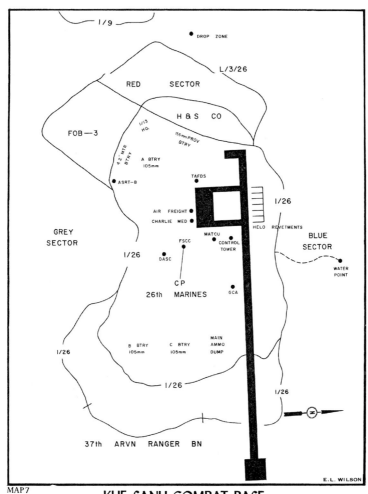

MAP 7 — KHE SANH COMBAT BASE

Chapter 1

-1986, Part I-

*"Be the first one on your block to
have your boy come home in a box."*
                              -*Country Joe McDonald*

Dear Mom,
Hello from Vietnam. How is everyone doing back home? You're all well, I hope. Hey, Mom, thanks for the letter. It was really great to hear from you. If you could, next time please include some pictures of the family. I miss you guys and it would sure be nice to see your faces again, even if it's only in a photograph.

So how's the weather in Philly? Has it snowed yet? The weather over here is lousy. During the day, it's sweltering hot, to the point that our clothes are soaked with sweat even when we're just sitting around doing nothing. Then, at night, the temperature drops so low that we have to wear extra poncho liners to keep from freezing. It rains all the time, too. Yesterday was the first time I saw the sun this week. The rain isn't all bad, though. At least when it rains I get the chance to clean up, which is nice since I haven't actually showered in more than a month. I also use the rain as an opportunity to fill my canteen with some much-needed drinking water. Still, despite the benefits it brings, three straight days of steady, driving rain is enough to make me dream about a parched desert. By the time the rain finally stops coming down, our bodies are all wrinkled and shriveled up, like when you spend too much time in the bathtub, and our gear is rotten and mildewed and smells absolutely horrible.

As bad as the weather is, the bugs are even harder to take — especially the mosquitoes. They say the North Vietnamese don't have an air force, but you could have fooled me. These bugs eat us alive, and the little bit of repellent we have does nothing to help. In addition to the mosquitoes, it seems like there are thousands of biting flies persistently swarming everywhere, feasting on us like buzzards on road kill.

Speaking of feasting, I think what I'm most looking forward to when I finally get stateside is a hot, home-cooked meal. Right about now, there isn't anything I wouldn't do for some of your ham and cabbage. All we ever have to eat are C-rations, and in comparison to them, most anything would taste better. Even then, we still don't get to eat three square meals a day. All our supplies, including the basic essentials like food and water, are very difficult to come by. Between the constant patrolling and the meager food rations, I think I've lost almost fifteen pounds since arriving in-country.

Promise me you won't get all worried, but I have to tell you about a close call that I had this past week. It happened while my squad was on a routine patrol in the jungle surrounding the base. Our unit was making really slow progress because the jungle was dense and we were hacking our way through the trees with machetes. After cutting a path for what must have been several hours, we came upon a clearing in the tree line. Just as soon as we moved forward into the clearing, some NVA popped up from out of nowhere and started shooting at us. Everyone in the unit dropped to the ground to take cover, and we all began returning fire. Next thing I knew, as I was lying there, trying to jam a fresh magazine into my M-16, a grenade came flying through the trees and landed only a few feet from me. I instinctively rolled away, turned my back to the grenade, and braced myself for the explosion. But thank God, the pin wasn't pulled. If the idiot who threw it had been smart enough to pull the pin out of the grenade, I probably wouldn't have gotten out of the way in time. I keep counting my blessings that I wasn't hurt. What sucks is that not everyone was so lucky. When the shooting started, our point man Billy took several rounds in the chest and died before we could get him a bird.

No matter how hard we try to defeat the enemy, I feel like the situation is getting worse around here, not better. It seems as though every day, somebody else on the base is killed or injured. Besides Billy, my friend Tommy was killed two days ago, shot dead by a sniper. Just this morning, some kid who hadn't been in-country more than a week, and who didn't look a day over eighteen, stepped on a land mine and blew off his leg. He was so new that I never even learned his name. The good news is that he will live and get the hell out of here, but he will spend the rest of his life as a cripple.

Even those of us who have somehow avoided being killed or injured have not escaped the brutality of this war. We're all physically and mentally shaken from what we have been through. Personally, I don't think I've had more than a few hours of sleep at a time in months. We live like rats burrowed in the dirt, and we reek of urine, blood, and gunpowder. We are covered in cuts and bruises, and our bodies continually ache. There is always a layer of dirt coating our bodies. We all smoke way too many cigarettes. Blisters have almost destroyed our feet, and everyone suffers from the obligatory cases of diarrhea and jock itch. Otherwise, we're fine.

One way I try to get through all this is by making sure to say a prayer every night for my buddies and me. I find it ironic, though, that I'm praying to a God in whom I have very little faith anymore. It is hard to have faith in God after witnessing the ugliness I have seen here. Recently, to help pass the time, I found myself doing a lot of soul searching. What I am coming to realize is that war is wrong. I know now that there is no point to it, to all the senseless death and destruction. Still, I keep on fighting because, despite my newfound beliefs, I also recognize that this war is not going to end just because that's what I want. And no matter what, above everything else, I must survive.

Still, Mom, to be truthful, I don't know how much more of this place I can handle. Sometimes I just sit and shake uncontrollably, my hands trembling and my ears ringing from the constant gunfire. I try to hold myself together, to not crack under the pressure. I even cry to myself sometimes, although I don't dare let anyone else know about that. Marines aren't supposed to cry. Marines are supposed to be strong. I'm trying hard to be strong, I swear, but it's just so damn difficult.

Sometimes I imagine us acting like scared children hiding in a closet from a thunderstorm. All the while, though, I feel like we're becoming hardened and emotionless, ready to walk right into the eye of the storm without even flinching. The craziest thing about it is that if I didn't know better, I'd think these reactions were those of an old man who had suffered a lifetime of tragedy and hardship. I mean, can you believe I'm expressing myself like this and am only eighteen years old? Just saying it, "eighteen years old," sounds so young. An eighteen-year-old shouldn't have to witness all the dreadful things I have seen over here. For that matter, no one should, regardless of his or her age. What I'm living through is something I wouldn't wish upon anyone.

However, the worst part of everything that I am experiencing is what happens when I close my eyes to try to get a few precious hours of sleep. When I am finally asleep, I dream terrifying dreams filled with ghosts. I see the ghosts of my friends—eighteen and nineteen-year-old kids who died way too young. I see the ghosts of civilians caught in the crossfire. I see the ghost of a North Vietnamese soldier whose brains I watched get driven through the back of his head by machine gun fire. But the most frightening ghost I see, the one I am absolutely petrified of, is that of the grim reaper. When I dream, I catch a glimpse of his deep, piercing smile and pearly white eyes staring out at me from underneath his black hood. I imagine him trying to reach out to me, mocking me, trying to take my life. Fortunately, in my dreams I'm able to find the power to fight back. But when I awake in a cold sweat, it becomes time for me to find the strength to fight him off for real.

Mom, I promise you that I won't let him get me. I promise that I'm not coming home to you in a box. I won't let them give you a flag. I want to survive. I want to see you again. I want to make it home from this godforsaken war, a war that I now know I never should have joined. It is just one of the many difficult lessons that this war has helped me understand. Too bad they are lessons I was unable to learn in some other, less painful way. However, of all the lessons this war has taught me, I think the most important is that . . .

. . . Life is a flickering flame that can, at anytime, be extinguished by the gentle, blowing breath of fate.

—

Dan's left hand tightened around the neck of the nearly empty bottle of beer now propped upon his left leg. On the floor, in front of the living room couch on which he now sat, were nearly another dozen freshly emptied bottles. The brown paper bag in which the beer had been wrapped, and that earlier had appeared so crisp and new, lay crumpled at his feet. On a small table in front of him was an almost empty pack of cigarettes and an overflowing ashtray. In his lap sat a jet-black telephone, his right hand cradling the receiver. Between the middle and index fingers of the same hand, a cigarette burned. Smoke from the cigarette drifted gently into the air. Staring deep into the dark black plastic surface of the phone, Dan was reminded of the many nights he spent in Vietnam in the pitch dark while assigned to a listening post. The thought made him shudder.

As Dan continued staring through the blackness of the phone, a glint of light reflected off the surface. The image thrown off by the light triggered the memory of a photograph he had once seen—that of a Buddhist monk who had committed an act of self-immolation on a Saigon street more then 20 years earlier. Now it was Dan's skin that felt like it might be on fire. He recalled that his own personal "gas can," a steel remnant from his days in-country, had been stored for years deep in the bowels of his basement. It was stowed away in a metal lockbox that sat in a drawer of an antique oak bureau, along with some tattered photographs from the war and an old police uniform. Chills ran up his spine at the thought.

As he took another drink from the bottle, his mind continued to race. His attention was focused deep inside his mind, on personally hurtful thoughts. There, in the inner depths of his psyche, a memory from the war triggered what had become a recurring mental picture of his own death. The images were crystal clear. Dan assumed that only events similar to those he had experienced during the years of his life following enlistment in the Marines were powerful enough to unlock this innermost part of the human brain. The backdrop for these images was a dark jungle of which Dan desired no part. He shuddered again, not wanting to consider the unthinkable possibilities.

The year was 1986. For the past eighteen years, Dan had lived with the memories of Vietnam. Each day, whether awake or asleep, he replayed in his head the horrors and carnage of the war. He lived with the gruesome memories of the untold number of corpses he had seen, both of friends and of enemies. He wrestled with the memory of seeing one of the best friends he ever knew lying dead, the top of his head missing. He often recalled that he had witnessed one of the most stunning places he ever laid eyes upon being ravaged and destroyed by bullets, rockets, bombs, fires, and Agent Orange. He had struggled to forget about the painful and horrendous events, the lives he may have taken, and those he had seen taken by others.

Dan tried to start over after returning home from the war in 1968. He had married in 1973, but the marriage ended less than two years later, solely because of his own mistakes. Caitlin had been a wonderful wife, and he had screwed up terribly. After years of working dead-end jobs or being unemployed, he finally found meaningful, steady work in

1976 as a police officer with the City of Philadelphia. In 1979, he married his second wife, Gloria. Michael was born almost two years later, and Robert arrived three years after that. On the surface, things were going relatively smoothly, but under the surface, life was in turmoil. Dan was always depressed, and he turned to alcohol for relief from reality. The excessive drinking only pushed him further into his depressed shell.

Consumed with what the doctors called "survivor's guilt," his thoughts reverted continually to friends he had loved and lost. He dwelled on the memories of friends who had died, and contemplated what he could have done differently to help save their lives. Dan wanted to know, more than anything else, why so many of his friends died and he had not. Why hadn't it been his blood that had stained red the stunningly green Vietnam landscape?

On top of the depression and guilt, there was the anger he felt. Mad at the world about the war and the needless killing that had occurred, the harsh realities of life had become too much for him to deal with successfully. With no suitable outlet for his emotions, he took out his anger and sporadic rage on others. There were repeated arguments and confrontations with both friends and strangers alike, and he exhibited a total lack of patience in dealing with people. Dan didn't trust anyone, and his paranoia was also marked by a general suspiciousness that prompted him to repeatedly glance over his shoulder to see who might be watching. Dan didn't show much concern for his own welfare or that of anyone else. He drove his car like a madman, taking unnecessary chances and risks, and otherwise lived life with reckless abandon. Not surprisingly, his behavior negatively affected his relationship with Gloria and their children. As the severe realities he faced exceeded what Dan was capable of handling, he turned more and more to alcohol. His life became a vicious cycle.

Unfortunately, no one cared about his problems. Nobody gave a damn about the Vietnam veterans. The American government did not care. The American public did not care. Even Dan's own friends and family seemed apathetic. No one cared that his often near-lunatic behavior had caused his first marriage to disintegrate and that he had given up on trying to make it work and had walked out on his wife, or that his sister, his own flesh and blood, had stopped talking to him because he had fought in the war. Nobody cared about the scars, both physical and emotional, that still lingered. Nobody wanted to hear about how, after years of trying to work things out, his second wife, Gloria, had given up the struggle and moved away with their two children.

Still seated on the living room couch, deep in his mind Dan visualized the fiery orange and red explosion of a muzzle flash, and then everything went dark. Dan's head jerked up and backward, his eyes opening wide. Sweat trickled off his forehead. He quickly put the bottle of beer to his lips and reached for another cigarette, trying desperately to control his emotions. He remained glued to the couch, all too aware that the stairwell to the basement, at the foot of which was the oak bureau, was but a short walk to the other side of the house. Dan's tired hands gripped the phone more tightly. Looking down at the smooth, dark plastic receiver, he realized his options were limited, and that the only way out for him tonight was to use the phone. Dan took a deep breath and closed his eyes, and as he did, all his memories drifted through his mind like a soft, cool fall breeze.

Chapter 2

-The Summer of 1967, Part 1: Boot Camp-

"Almost everything is easier to get into, than out of."
                                                    -Agnes Allen

Daniel John Sullivan was born in February 1949, the second of three children to John and Christine Sullivan. He grew up in a diverse working-class neighborhood of Philadelphia, composed of one-way streets and row homes. The owners of these homes typically worked in one of Philadelphia's many textile factories. It was a patriotic community—on every porch flew an American flag—and most of the older men, including Dan's father, were veterans of World War II.

John Sullivan served in the Army Air Corps, and spent time as a prisoner of war after his plane was shot down over Germany. As a result of the combination of post-war stress, heavy drinking, and the overwhelming responsibility of raising a family, John abandoned his wife while Dan was still a young child. Christine, left to support Dan, his older brother Patrick, and younger sister Emily on her own, was forced to work long hours in Philadelphia's textile factories. The bulk of the responsibility for taking care of the three Sullivan children consequently fell on their grandmother. She was, like Dan's father, a heavy drinker, and verbally abusive toward the children.

Following John's abandonment of the family, the closest person Dan had to a father was his Uncle Jim. Also a veteran of World War II, Jim loved rooting for the Philadelphia Phillies, and on occasion took Dan to baseball games at old Connie Mack Stadium. As best he could, Uncle Jim treated Dan like his own son, serving as a role model and always making himself available to give advice or to lend an ear.

Dan grew up a normal teenager for his time. He was of average height and build, although he may have tended a little to the skinny side. He had smooth brown hair, baby blue eyes, and a big grin complemented by silver dollar dimples. He was handsome enough, and possessed charm, a sense of humor, a quick wit, and sometimes, an even quicker tongue. As a teenager, Dan attended a Catholic high school in Philadelphia. When not in school, chasing girls, or having a beer with his friends, he worked as a movie theatre usher and at a local gas station pumping gas. With money saved from working, he bought a 1960 Roman-white Chevy Impala that became his pride and joy. He liked John Wayne movies, the Rolling Stones, and baseball, his favorite team, of course, being the Phillies.

Although his brother Patrick had done well in high school and went on to attend Temple University, even paying his own tuition, Dan had neither the money, motivation, or grades to attend college. Despite being an intelligent boy with generally good common sense, Dan never became an accomplished student, due at least in part to a mild case of dyslexia, which was not diagnosed until much later in life. He had trouble concentrating on his studies, and typically received poor grades. This resulted in a deep frustration with school.

Instead of continuing on to college, Dan decided to enlist in the United States Marine Corps. Since many of the adult men Dan knew were military veterans, and some of his friends were already on active duty overseas, to Dan, enlistment seemed the natural thing to do. In February of 1967, only days after celebrating his eighteenth birthday, and with high school graduation only a few months away, Dan went to a Marine Corps recruiting station near his aunt's home in the Philadelphia suburb of Willow Grove. After submitting proof of age, Dan officially enlisted in the Marines, his active duty status delayed until three days after his high school graduation in June.

June 12, 1967
Journal Entry

I graduated from high school today, and you know what? Good riddance! I've been waiting four months for this day, ever since signing on with the Corps. I mean, I really couldn't stand that place. Besides, I have so many better things to anticipate with high school behind me. Now I have the chance to move on with my life and become a man. Think about it. I'm eighteen. Grown up, out of high school, and on my own. I'm ready to take on the world, live life, and experience all the independence and freedom that come from being out of the house. In addition, it's no secret that high school proved to be a really bad experience for me. What a drag it was. I guess hanging out with my friends was fun, but I was never interested in actually being in class, and certainly never got very good grades. And let's not even get started on the nuns!

Now, though, I won't have to deal with any of that stuff ever again. Finally, I have something to which I can look forward. Enlisting may just prove to be one of the best steps I've ever taken. Think about it for a second. If I don't enlist, I'm a high school graduate with no job lined up, nowhere to go, nothing to do, and no real skills I can use. But by becoming a Marine, I'll travel to faraway and exotic places, build myself into a monster of a person, and as a bonus, I'll learn a skill, like a mechanical trade, that I can apply in the workplace. Then, once my enlistment period is up, I'll be able to take that skill and get a job. That's everything I ever wanted or needed.

I know Mom is all worried that something bad could happen to me, but I don't see why. Plenty of men in the neighborhood served in the military, and they are all doing fine. And let's face facts for a minute. Between my grades and Mom's income, I wasn't going to college anyhow. And with the lack of trade skills I have now, I'll never find a job that will amount to anything.

Anyway, tonight I'm heading down to the Jersey shore with Mike and Joey for one last weekend of fun before I enter the Marines. Then, on Monday morning, I'm off to the real world. It all can't come soon enough.

—

When Dan enlisted in February 1967, Vietnam already had a significant American troop presence. The ground war, however, had not yet amounted to much more than a series of small skirmishes between American forces and disorganized North Vietnamese troops and South Vietnamese communists (also known as the Viet Cong). Fighting was still several months away from escalating to the stage that would make the conflict the focus of the entire world. The potential consequences of volunteering to join a branch of the US military that could eventually become a major factor in an ever-escalating war did not worry Dan. Then again, why should he be concerned? When Dan signed up, the Marine recruiting officer explained to him that he would be fixing trucks and helicopters, not fighting on the front lines. After all, Dan surmised, how dangerous could it be to repair a transmission?

June 17, 1967
Dear Mom,

    I'm writing this letter sitting on a clunky yellow school bus, similar to the kind I used to take to school every day. The bus is filled with other recruits like me, and we're traveling somewhere through the middle of South Carolina. I count about thirty other guys on the bus, and I don't believe any of them have said more than three words the whole trip. The lack of conversation is probably due to a combination of nervousness and fatigue. It's 2:30 in the morning, and while I should be completely exhausted, there are just too many thoughts bouncing around in my head for me to close my eyes. I'm so anxious with anticipation that I'm barely able to sit still, let alone fall asleep. I wish I could see the landscape along the bus route, because I assume I would find it fascinating and it might relax me, but it's just too dark outside to make anything out. I keep thinking about the plane ride down, too. I'll tell you, it was something else. As many times as I have seen airplanes in the sky, it was a big thrill to actually get to fly in one.

    Mom, the real reason I'm writing is that I need to share my thoughts about a very sensitive subject. I know it's your opinion that my joining the Marines was a mistake, but I hope you understand why I don't agree. Please try to appreciate that it was something I needed to do for myself. I had to get out of Philadelphia, go away and discover the world. I expect to become a man soon. I'll get some real life experience and learn how to be a mechanic. Before too long I'll return to Philly, get a respectable job, and make you proud. Besides, we both know there's no way I was going to college. This will be good for me, you'll see. Just as the recruiter said, this is going to be the best thing I'll ever do.

    Well, I'm beginning to get a little tired. Wait a minute. I see something on the horizon. There are lights. It looks like it could be a military base. This has to be our destination, so I'm going to end now. I'll write as much as possible. Say hello to Emily and Patrick for me.

    Love,
    Daniel

June 22, 1967
Dear Mike,

    Hey, man, how's the neighborhood? Is everything holding up without me? I can't believe it. No more high school. No more classes. I love it! Hey, was senior weekend a blast, or what? It was unreal how much I drank, and how much you puked. Anyway, you can't begin to imagine what I've gotten myself into down here. To put it simply, boot camp sucks. Matter of fact, it is hell. The weather is hot as can be, and unbearably muggy. It's worse than a Philadelphia summer with all the concrete and hot asphalt. The temperature is in the 90s, with 100% humidity, and the mosquitoes are as big as small birds.

Before I forget, I have to tell you about my crazy first night here. I got off the plane in Charleston, and from there took a bus with a bunch of other new recruits to my current location, a base called Parris Island—a big Marine Corps recruit depot out in the middle of nowhere. When we arrived, the bus pulled up and sat on the blacktop for what seemed like an eternity. It was still and dark outside, and my clothes were sticking to me from the mugginess. I began to think we might just sit there all night when a drill instructor came onto the bus. Initially, he very calmly introduced himself, like a schoolteacher presenting himself to his students on the first day of class. I was almost waiting for him to turn around and write his name on a blackboard. Then, without warning, he went absolutely ballistic.

"You ladies have ten seconds to get off this bus!" he screamed at the top of his lungs.

I swear, Mike, he was yelling louder than anyone I'd ever heard before. Man, if anyone had been sleeping before, they weren't now. We all shot out of our seats, and started knocking each other down trying to make our way off the bus. There were even guys who climbed over seats and jumped out of the windows, that's how afraid we were. When we finally all made it off the bus onto the blacktop, there were another half-dozen rabid drill instructors waiting to pounce on us. They made us line up and stand at attention on yellow footprints painted on the ground. The whole time they had us on the blacktop they were cursing and hollering things like, "Move it, you fucking hog bait," and "Welcome to hell, you shitheads."

This one instructor got right up in my face and started shrieking, "Don't you move, you asshole."

Man, I was frightened. Spit was flying out of his mouth, and I could see the veins on his neck popping. He kept yelling at me, screaming threats such as, "If you so much as flinch, I'll bash in your skull, you pathetic piece of shit."

Bro, I was so terrified I couldn't have moved even if I had wanted. And I'm glad I couldn't, too. Some guys started looking around or talking, and the drill instructors got right in their faces. This kid next to me said something to one of the instructors and got punched right in his gut. He started dry heaving right there on the spot. I didn't dare look, but I could hear him gasping for air. Finally, after standing on the blacktop for much longer than made any sense, especially given the hour, we were taken to get our heads shaved and then ordered to our barracks. Even though I was exhausted, it took me a good half-hour to calm down before I could fall asleep. I'm not sure I've ever been that scared in my life.

I got maybe two hours of sleep, and at about 0600, we awakened to screaming from more drill instructors. We were immediately corralled into the middle of our barracks, and I was assigned to my platoon. We were then introduced to our platoon drill instructors. These drill instructors turned out to be even worse than those who greeted us when the bus arrived. They are the toughest sons of bitches you'd ever meet, the kind of people you could imagine ripping the heart out of someone's chest. I'm not going to cross their paths, no way. Anyhow, we have spent the last couple of days receiving our gear and taking medical tests. Damn, it's almost lights out. I have to go. I'll write again.

Take care,
Danny

July 10, 1967
Journal Entry

Boot camp is a lot tougher than I ever expected. Our only purpose for living, as far as our drill instructors are concerned, is to become Marines. Anything else is irrelevant. Seven days a week, practically twenty-four hours a day, we are taught the basics of how to become and act like a US Marine. We learn how to march, take orders, fire weapons, and toughen ourselves up. We're put through all types of physical training exercises, including obstacle courses, strength tests, and instructional hand-to-hand combat. The most grueling exercises are the daylong, twenty-mile hikes, carrying sixty-pound rucksacks on our backs.

However, where we focus the greatest amount of time is learning how to fire our rifles. I never fired a weapon before boot camp, but now, with all the instruction and practice on the firing range, I'm actually becoming a fairly accurate shot. I have worked really hard at improving my marksmanship, perhaps because I guess it's important to be able to take pride in being competent in at least one skill. I think most everyone can claim a level of expertise in one field or another. Some people are successful athletes, others have an ability with numbers, while still others get high grades for screaming orders at Marine recruits. I guess my one thing to be good at is firing a rifle.

July 14, 1967
Journal Entry

If there's one aspect that I hate most about basic training, without a doubt it is the hell we are always catching from our drill instructors. Many of these guys are old WWII and Korean War vets who know what it takes to prepare for and fight a war, and the Marine Corps has tasked them with teaching us all about discipline, respect, and battlefield toughness.

There are three assigned to our platoon, and they control every phase of our lives. They tell us when to wake up in the morning, when to eat, when to go to sleep, and when to make every other move you could possibly think of. I can't even take a piss without their permission. They have instilled the fear of God in every recruit in the platoon, including me. Our instructors are hard-core, hard-nosed Marines, and they don't take shit from anyone. They make the nuns from Catholic school seem like kind, little old ladies.

I honestly believe our drill instructors are here to mentally torture us. They treat us like dogs, as if we're the scum of the earth, all so they can break us down and build us back up into mean fighting machines. They're constantly screaming orders, with every other word out of their mouths being a four-letter word. On top of that, they're always mentally tearing down the recruits, calling us demeaning names and getting in our faces every time we do something not exactly to their liking. Even though they aren't supposed to hit us, they threaten to do it anyhow. And if anyone screws up, he better watch out, because these guys don't hold back.

Staff Sergeant Kurtz and Buck Sergeant Peters are the toughest of the bunch. I'm not kidding when I say that these two guys are real crazy Marines. Sometimes I have the feeling they get pleasure out of putting down the recruits. They'll beat up on people for screwing up a minor detail or performing a task too slowly. Other times they'll go at a recruit because they decide that he is weak, or they simply don't like his attitude. Most often, though, it seems they are doing it solely for fun, or because they're bored and looking for something to keep themselves entertained. For example, we were running an obstacle course the other day through a muddy field, and one of the recruits slipped right in front of the instructors. Kurtz got so mad at the sight of him falling that he lost his head.

"Get up, you idiot," he screamed. "Get up before I kick your ass."

Then, as the recruit was trying to stand up, Kurtz put his boot in the middle of the guy's back and pushed him face first back into the mud. I mean, how is he supposed to get up if Kurtz keeps kicking him?

It's not just physical abuse, either. Kurtz and Peters also like to humiliate people. There was one recruit who was eventually discharged because of a kidney problem, but before being diagnosed he always had to go to the bathroom. This annoyed Peters to no end, and so for fun, he would stick this poor kid in front of the platoon and make him piss all over himself.

July 19, 1967

Second Battalion Recruit Platoon had messed up big-time, and was about to face the consequences. After being worked relentlessly for days and moving extra sluggishly all morning, the last straw for the drill instructors came when the recruits did a poor job of cleaning their barracks. As punishment, each member of the platoon was ordered to fill up his green canvas duffel bag with all his gear. They were then ordered to stand in front of their bunks while fully extending the bags, which now weighed roughly sixty pounds, high over their heads. As the recruits struggled to comply, Kurtz and Peters paced back and forth through the barracks, looking for guys who were dropping their arms, waiting for the slightest movement so they could swoop down on their prey.

Dan was exhausted. It had already been a long, physically draining day, and it was taking all his remaining strength to keep the duffel held over his head. Finally, the weight became more than he could bear, and his arms momentarily budged. They did not move much, perhaps only a couple of inches, but it was enough that Kurtz noticed. From across the room, Kurtz made a beeline straight to Dan, and without pausing, punched him square in the belly. Dan's stomach tightened as he doubled over and fell hard to the ground, coughing, choking for air, and grasping his mid-section.

As he buckled over, Dan dropped his duffel, which landed on Kurtz's spit-shined shoes. One of the first rules all new recruits quickly learned at boot camp was that they should never mess with a Marine drill instructor's spit-shines. They were taught that a Marine's spit-shine is sacred, and represents everything good and right with the Corps. To obtain the perfect spit-shine takes time, patience, practice, and dedication, and all honorable United States Marines, especially Marine drill instructors, take very seriously the responsibility of ensuring that their shoes maintain a flawless shine. Any blemish is viewed with personal embarrassment. When Dan's duffel fell on Kurtz's shoes, it broke all those rules, and Kurtz took the matter personally.

"How dare you scuff up my spit-shine, you maggot," Kurtz screamed in rage as he delivered a sharp kick to Dan's mid-section.

Not satisfied that he had taught Dan his lesson, Kurtz bent over and reached for Dan's uniform. As his left hand grabbed the collar of Dan's shirt, an open-palmed smack from his right hand found its way to Dan's face. Finally content that he had instilled the appropriate degree of Marine discipline into Dan, Kurtz let go of his collar. With no strength left in his body, Dan's head fell to the floor with a resounding thud. And then, as if the incident had never happened, Kurtz turned and walked away, looking for the next recruit upon whom he could impose his own brand of schooling.

July 22, 1967
Dear Mom,

Sorry it's taken so long to write, but there's really not much time for letters. The instructors constantly have us doing something, whether it's training, cleaning the barracks, or doing push-ups. It never stops with the orders and the commands. Even when we get a chance to sleep, it's only because we are told to do so. I have had some opportunities for making friends with the other guys in my platoon. Believe it or not, there are two other recruits here from Philly. One is named Will, and the other Jamal. I share a bunk with a guy by the name of George Brown. You should see him. He's a huge kid who is tough as nails. I swear, he looks like the picture-perfect Marine. He's a nice guy, too, and because he is so likeable, everyone feels comfortable kidding him about the way he talks. What I mean is that, being from Ohio, he has different words for things than we do. Like, for example, he calls soda "pop" and sneakers "tennis shoes." It's really comical to hear him speak.

Anyway, the weather is still hot and muggy, and the food is terrible, but I'll survive. I knew I wasn't coming here for a vacation. Well, less than a month until I see you again. I can't wait for boot camp graduation. I hope you can make it down for the ceremony.

Love,
Daniel

August 2, 1967
Journal Entry

Those drill instructors finally took it a step too far. One of the recruits in the platoon messed up, so Kurtz decided to punish everyone by playing his favorite game, which is a little thing he likes to call "Let's Play Jesus Christ."

It all started when Kurtz came barging into the barracks while we were cleaning. He slammed the door real loudly so we knew he was there, and began screaming at the top of his lungs.

"You shit-bird pansies continue to screw up like a bunch of stupid retards. Haven't you assholes learned a friggin' thing? I guess not. Well, one way or another, you're going to learn to get it right. Now, c'mon, everyone on their racks. Let's play Jesus Christ."

With those words, the whole platoon apprehensively headed for their bunk beds. Everyone stepped onto the end of the lower bunk and faced outwards, with our backs pressed against the frame. We then had to stick our arms through the end rails on the top bunk and let our feet dangle toward the ground, so that we were hanging helpless, our arms pinned painfully behind us. Kurtz and Peters love to see us in this position because we are wide open and they can take full advantage of our vulnerability. I mean, they really seem to take pleasure in striding around the barracks, getting right up in guys' faces, screaming and cursing and taking shots at our defenseless bodies.

On this particular round of "Let's Play Jesus Christ," Kurtz and Peters went to work on one poor kid who they both disliked even more than the rest of us. I'm not sure why, but from the first day of boot camp they never cared for him. It's possible they thought he was kind of a "momma's boy" who was too soft, or that he was not aggressive or motivated enough to be a Marine. Either way, I suppose for no particular reason other than they felt like it, on this occasion they threw several punches to his stomach and punched him in the arms just like schoolyard bullies. Meanwhile, the whole time this is going on, the guy was yelling and crying, screaming for them to stop, snot was bubbling out of his nose, and tears were running down his face.

Unfortunately, by the time the two of them finally backed away, it was too late. They hurt the kid badly enough so that nerves in one of his arms were injured, and we hear he may lose the use of the arm. Afterwards, there was a big investigation, but of course, when the military police asked, none of us saw a thing. Truthfully, we witnessed too much, and didn't want to suffer the same fate if we ratted. But even without an incriminating word from any of the recruits, the MPs pieced together enough information to build a case. The word is circulating that Kurtz and Peters are both going to be court-martialed, and will probably be kicked out of the Marines.

August 20, 1967

Full of curiosity and anticipation, the recruits quickly circled the Marine sergeant who had just entered their barracks. As he spoke, his booming voice carried through the squad bay.

"Jefferson, Levi A."

"Yes, sir," Private Jefferson responded. It was the reply of a boy about to become a Marine.

"0300, Infantry." The sergeant called the next name on his list. "Leroy, Cory M."

Another proud and prompt, "Yes, sir."

"0300, Infantry. Gregory, Eric E."

"Yes, sir."

"0300, Infantry. Sullivan, Daniel J."

"Yes, sir," Dan replied anxiously.

"0300, Infantry."

Infantry? What the hell was this sergeant talking about? Dan was stunned. He could not believe what he was hearing. After a moment, his stomach began to feel a little sick. Dan had anticipated that he would be assigned to work as a mechanic when he graduated boot camp. Now, suddenly, he was being assigned to duty in the infantry. The MOS he had just received was "0300 due for Westpack." In Marine speak, it meant he was being posted to Vietnam to fight on the front lines. However, he would not be going alone.

Every Marine in his platoon, except for a lucky few who had somehow managed to draw assignments to MP school or sea duty, was also receiving an MOS of 0300. Instead of driving trucks or working on helicopters, as the great bulk of the recruits expected they would be doing following completion of basic training, most would find themselves on the front lines of a war that resembled nothing of what it had been only months earlier. A war that as recently as May had involved no more than random, minor skirmishes was escalating dramatically.

"But, sir," one recruit spoke up, "I'm supposed to be fueling helicopters."

"Sir, they told me I'd be driving trucks," another recruit said.

"Sir, I thought I was going to be fixing Jeeps."

It was the same complaint all around. Virtually every recruit was expecting to graduate and learn a trade, and each wanted to know how he had gone from becoming a mechanic to serving in the infantry. Confronted with this line of questioning, the instructor, likely all too aware of the fate that some of those who now stood in front of him were to meet, sounded almost sympathetic in his response.

"Sorry about that, guys, but we're fighting a war, and we need people in the infantry."

—

And this was true. By the time of Dan's graduation from Parris Island, the Vietnam conflict had become a full-scale war making front-page news in every major newspaper in the country. The average number of American soldiers killed each month had nearly doubled from 477 in 1966 to 816 in 1967.[1] In the prior year alone, the number of American troops in Vietnam had increased from 385,000 to 485,600, and 16,021 Americans had already been killed and another 99,762 injured.[2] Indeed, more and more servicemen needed to be replaced every day. It was a war that had grown more serious than most Americans initially imagined it would become, and it was only getting worse.

August 21, 1967
Journal Entry

I saw Mom today after the graduation ceremony. I told her about my MOS. She was upset, but wasn't surprised. She said she figured the military would do something like that.

Chapter 3

-Summer of '67, Part 2: Advanced Training-

"Made up my mind, make a new start.
Going to California with an aching in my heart."
    -Led Zeppelin, "Going to California"

August 23, 1967

Dan packed the last of his gear into the green locker, hung his duffel on a hook, and turned to survey the rest of the barracks. There were a few guys reading or writing letters, most likely to or from their mothers or girlfriends. Down at the other end of the barracks, several Marines were standing around discussing baseball, debating who was better—Mickey Mantle, Hank Aaron, or Willie Mays. Some Marines played cards on their bunks, while others tossed darts in the corner, using a makeshift dartboard fashioned out of a piece of cardboard. What particularly caught Dan's attention, however, was the music streaming from a radio a few bunks over, which Dan immediately determined to be some of the most god-awful music ever recorded.

"Hadn't this guy ever heard of the Rolling Stones?" Dan thought to himself. With nothing better to do, he decided to find out.

"Hey, man, what's going on?" Dan asked as he strolled over to the apparent owner of the radio.

"Not much. What's going on with you?" The reply came in a thick southern accent, impossible to miss.

"What's your name?"

"Robbie. Robbie Cassidy." Again, the thick southern accent resounded.

"I'm Danny Sullivan. Good to meet you, man," Dan responded, holding out his hand. "What's with the accent, bro? I mean, what part of the country are you from?"

"I'm from Texas. Little town called Silsbee," Robbie proudly informed Dan.

"Texas, huh? Well, that would explain the music, I guess."

"Don't you like country music?" Robbie asked, a slight smile rising from the corner of his mouth.

"Not really," Dan replied, returning the smile. "Actually, I hate that stuff. Personally, I like the Stones and Bob Dylan."

"Bob Dylan? Yeah, I think I've heard of him. Well, we'll get you used to liking country music soon enough," Robbie laughed. "So whereabouts are you from?"

"Philadelphia."

"Philadelphia. That's a big city, isn't it? What's it like living in a big city?"

"Tell you what," Dan said. "Turn off that music, let's grab a beer, and I'll tell you all about it."

Robbie smiled widely. "Now that," he said, "is a good idea."

August 30, 1967

Dear Mom,

Thanks again for coming to graduation. It was great to see you, even if it was only for a few hours. Well, I'm through my first week of infantry training, with only two more to go. After that, they tell us we're getting a period of leave to go home, or do whatever. I'm planning to use the time to come back to Philly and visit. I'm actually looking forward to it, too. I think I need a break from military life for a couple of days.

Anyway, infantry training is a lot different than basic training. For one thing, North Carolina isn't as hot as South Carolina, and there are far fewer mosquitoes. The biggest difference, though, is that having gotten through basic training, I'm finally considered a full-fledged Marine. Now I'm actually treated like a human being again. There's so much more freedom here, and I even get a little time to kick back, relax, and catch my breath. That's something we never had during basic. It's not as if we can leave base and go into town whenever we want, but things are better. There's even beer here for us to drink.

Even though the mood is more laid back here than it was at Parris Island, it's still not all fun and games. There's a lot of instruction taking place, most of it centered on learning how to fight what the military calls a "conventional war." We're instructed in all sorts of military tactics, like performing maneuvers and assembling into formations used in battle settings. We're also learning how to engage in house-to-house combat, in case we have to fight in a city, and jungle warfare since, of course, Vietnam is mostly one big jungle. A cool thing about this training is that we're being introduced to new weapons. At basic, all they taught us to shoot was an M-14, but in Vietnam we will be issued M-16s. Here we're being shown how the M-16 works, how to break it down, and clean it, and we've even had the chance to fire off a couple of rounds. Later, we're supposed to learn how to use heavier stuff, like grenade and rocket launchers.

As for me, I'm doing okay. I met this kid Robbie, who lives in my barracks. He's eighteen, like me, but he's from the middle-of-nowhere in Texas. He does weird things, like listen to country music, and he talks with this strange southern accent, but he's a real nice guy, and we've become good friends.

When you saw me at graduation, you mentioned I looked like I had lost some weight, so I'm trying to eat more. However, I still can't seem to put on any pounds. It must be the heat. Oh, by the way, please ask Uncle Jim to send me some box scores from the newspapers. I still don't find out much about how the Phillies are doing, even though we are allowed to read the papers again. I know they're out of the pennant race, but they're still the Phillies. Well, I'm going to sign off. See you soon.

Love,
Daniel

September 2, 1967

With everyone having filed onto the bleachers and taken their seats, the overhead lights powered down. With the lights off, the shadows of the moths that had earlier danced across the beams of light disappeared, and the Marines were enveloped in complete darkness. There was nothing to see, and nothing moved. Even the moon seemed to have disappeared for the moment. The late summer evening was still and mostly quiet, the only sounds the occasional distant rattle of a summer locust and the spooky creaking of the aging metal bleachers. Then, suddenly, the sky became a blaze of light, as if thousands of fireworks were ignited simultaneously.

Night turned into day as countless rounds of military ammunition streaked overhead. Explosions, loud cracks from the firing of guns, and whistling bullets piercing the night sky filled the air, ripping through the silence. The sights and sounds, which at first startled the Marines assembled on the bleachers, soon held them in awe. For nearly a full minute, they sat and watched as an entire Marine rifle platoon, secretly camouflaged in front of the bleachers, fired several thousand rounds of ammunition from their weapons.

Adding to the amazing spectacle was the factor that every single round fired was a tracer round, which contained chemicals that caused the path of the bullet to be visible at night. The tracers illuminated the pitch-black field with a green, almost entrancing glow as they flew through the air, leaving the impression that the horizon was covered with swarms of fireflies.

Then, as suddenly as it had started, the shooting stopped. The sky again went black and silent, and the rifle platoon disappeared into the night. Even though the shooting had ceased, it seemed to Dan as if he could still see the tracers dancing in front of his eyes. The air was thick with the smell of gunpowder, and his ears were still ringing from the incredible noise the volley had produced. His heart beat more quickly than two minutes prior.

It was a tremendous display of firepower, one of the most impressive any of the assembled Marines had ever witnessed in person. "Hey, Robbie," Dan whispered, never taking his eyes off the area in front of the bleachers, hoping there might be more to come.

"Yeah, Dan?"

"We're gonna kick some ass."

―

The purpose of the exhibition, one that every Marine who went through infantry training experienced, was to show the impact of a rifle platoon using its full firepower to repel a North Vietnamese ground assault. This exercise was important for building the confidence of the Marines in themselves and their weapons, as it related to both their fighting ability and fire superiority. For all the physical training they were receiving, the Marines were also undergoing intense mental conditioning in preparation for combat. Whether through observing demonstrations like this, or as a result of their instructors only referring to the Vietnamese enemy as slants, dinks, and gooks, with each passing day the Marines were being instilled with the belief that they were superior to the North Vietnamese in every respect.

September 5, 1967

Dear Mike,

Hey, bro, what's going on? I'll be home in a couple of weeks, so get ready. We're going to do some serious damage while I'm around. Yo, man, let me tell you, Vietnam is going to be no problem. The NVA aren't going to know what the hell hit them. I mean, really, we have such superior firepower, and they are just running around in their pajamas with obsolete rifles. Our instructors tell us about how they are a backward people who talk all quick and funny and still live in the jungle, and about how uneducated and illiterate they are. I just don't see how they can match up to our military might. From what I have seen here, and based on what the Marines who have already been there tell us, the NVA and Viet Cong don't stand a chance. As I said, going over there won't be any problem. Anyway, I'll see you in a week and tell you more about everything.

Take care,
Danny

September 28, 1967

Weaving his way through the maze of airport terminals with family in tow, Dan felt like he was on the longest walk of his life. After a few wrong turns and several inquiries to airport employees for directions, he at last located the gate from which his plane would depart. Tired of lugging his heavy duffel, Dan dropped it on the ground, leaving his mother to watch it as he went to check in at the ticket counter. When he returned to his waiting family, Uncle Jim was the first to break the uncomfortable silence and start the last round of goodbyes.

"You take care of yourself, Danny, okay? Come back as soon as you can, and we'll go catch a Phillies game together."

"I will, Uncle Jim," Dan replied. "We'll go as soon as I get back." With that, the two shared a quick hug.

His mom, Christine, was next. She reached out and took Dan's hand. Squeezing it firmly, Christine moved closer and grabbed Dan, embracing him in a huge hug.

"Daniel," his mom said weakly, fighting back tears, "Didn't I tell you never to volunteer for anything?" Her question represented a futile attempt to make herself smile. Finally, a tear trickled down her cheek. As Dan reached up to wipe it away, Christine fumbled through her pocketbook looking for a tissue.

"Mom, please don't cry. You promised."

"I know I did, Daniel, it's, it's just—well—" She paused, searching for words. Dan hugged her tightly again. "It's just that first it was your father, and now you. You're only eighteen. You're so young, Daniel." Her voice trailed off into a whisper. "I mean, you're still just a child."

Dan nodded, but didn't say anything. He understood. It had been hard enough for his mother to deal with his father both during and after he returned from World War II, and now her son was being sent off to fight in a brand new war.

"Now boarding, Flight 105 for California."

It was Dan's flight. The moment for final goodbyes had arrived.

"Bye, Uncle Jim. You take it easy."

"Bye, Danny. Take care."

Dan turned to his mother. She was crying openly now. Dan felt himself beginning to lose his composure, too. He decided to make the final goodbye quick. He put his arms around his mother, and the two again hugged tightly.

"Be careful, Daniel. Please," his mother pleaded between sobs. "Please, please, please take care of yourself. Come home to me. I love you."

"I love you, too," Dan said softly as he kissed her on the cheek, picked up his duffel, and boarded the plane.

The flight was difficult for Dan. The scene at the airport had drained him emotionally, and a feeling of nervousness about what lay ahead began to creep into his gut. He made an effort to enjoy the in-flight movie, but paying attention proved impossible. To keep from becoming too upset about the prospect of soon being in Vietnam, Dan tried thinking about the fun he would have hanging with Robbie once he arrived in California. But after even that failed to cheer him up, Dan decided he could use a drink to help calm his nerves.

"Excuse me, ma'am," Dan said, stopping the stewardess.

"Yes? May I help you?"

"Could I get a beer, please?"

"Are you twenty-one? I'll need to see some identification."

"Come on, lady. I'm about to go to Vietnam to fight a war. Can't you cut me a break?"

"I'm sorry, but the law is the law," she responded unsympathetically as she walked away.

Dan thought that really sucked. He was old enough to die for his country, but not old enough to be served a beer.

October 15, 1967
Dear Mom,

I'm just writing to say hello while I have the chance. Things are a little hectic at the moment, so I don't know how much spare time I'll have for the next little while. In case you were wondering, I was assigned to the 3rd Marine Division at Camp Pendleton, California. Robbie, the guy from Texas that I told you about, was here when I arrived, and we have been hanging out a lot together. Can you believe some people never even showed? I guess they went to Canada instead. I'm just as worried as the next guy about going to Vietnam, but going AWOL never once crossed my mind. No matter how scared I am, I know that I have to do my duty and serve my country.

Right now, we're going through about two weeks of guerrilla warfare training. We're learning what we'll need to know about once we're in Vietnam, like offensive tactics and about how the enemy hides in the jungle and sets up ambushes in rice paddies. Well, it's almost chow time, so I'm going to head off to the mess hall. I'll write again soon. Say hello to everyone for me.

Love,
Daniel

November 11, 1967
Journal Entry

Tomorrow we leave for Okinawa, Japan, where we will spend a couple of days before our final departure for Vietnam. For our last night at Camp Pendleton, after dinner we went to an auditorium on base to watch a movie. Before the movie started, an officer, who must have been at least in his forties and looked very official, stood up in front of everyone and began speaking.

"Gentlemen," he announced in his best official-sounding military voice, "within days you will be in Vietnam. There will be no more learning exercises, no more mock raids, and no more training demonstrations. What you experience there will be the real thing. You must mentally prepare yourself for what you might encounter while in the battle zone. The gooks will do everything they can to make sure that you do not come home alive. What I'm saying is not meant to scare you, but to make you realize that when you confront those slant-eyed scum-of-the-earth North Vietnamese and Viet Cong, you should not hesitate for one moment to blow them away. It is quite simple. Do not be indecisive, because those bastards you are fighting against will not hesitate for one second to kill you. Men, good luck, and Godspeed."

With that, the lights dimmed, and the movie started. The film began with actual footage of combat in Vietnam, which was supposed to provide a sense of what it's really like on the front lines. Maybe because we figured we would see enough of the real thing in a couple of days, or maybe on account of us all being just a bunch of irresponsible teenagers, no one was really paying attention. Most of the audience was talking and joking around. We had all watched scenes on television of the rice paddies and helicopters flying over the jungle, and we had all seen enough John Wayne movies to know what a gunfight looked like.

However, about thirty seconds into the film, it cut to an unedited scene of fighting that was particularly violent and graphic. It showed a group of Marines somewhere in the jungle firing their weapons at unseen targets and scrambling around frantically. This was nothing like anything we had ever seen in a Hollywood movie. The battle was very intense, and the Marines seemed confused and really scared. The camera zoomed in on one particular cluster of Marines, and as it did, you could almost feel their fear. As the scene played out, all of a sudden, one of the Marines closest to the battlefield camera took a couple of rounds right in his chest. His uniform was torn apart from the impact, and he immediately slumped to the ground.

As I watched, stunned, I became very aware that the auditorium had fallen completely silent. The camera focused on the one soldier as he lay motionless on the ground. As blood dripped from his mouth, you could see that his eyes had rolled back into his head, and it was easy to imagine the holes in his body where he had been shot. Watching the scene, I suddenly had a feeling of, "Hey, this is for real," and at that moment, I was hit by the realization of what lay ahead in Vietnam.

Still, I'm honestly not all that worried about Vietnam. I know people die in war, and sure, I guess what I saw in the film was a little dose of reality, but that won't happen to me. Vietnam is not going to be the end of me. After all, I'm only eighteen, and way too young to die.

November 12, 1967

Dan and Robbie carried their trays of food over to a table where there were several empty seats, and sat down. The two had just arrived in Okinawa that afternoon, and both were starving after the long flight from California. As the Marines ate, noisy conversation and the sounds of utensils clanking against trays and plates filled the mess hall. Many of the Marines, including Dan and Robbie, would be receiving final medical check-ups and inoculation shots over the next three days, before leaving Japan for Vietnam.

"Hey, Robbie," Dan began to ask between mouthfuls of food. "Can you believe we're here for three days, and we don't get any liberty off the base? We're gonna be bored out of our minds. The least they could do is let us spend a night in town."

"You guys want to get into town?" a voice asked. The two Marines turned to the soldier sitting next to them.

"What was that?" asked Robbie.

"I overheard you guys talking about how you wanted to go have some fun. You know, get off base, and into town. Maybe to do some drinking? Well, if you're interested, there's a place along the perimeter where you can climb over the fence and the guards won't catch you. All you have to do is climb over and make sure you're not too drunk to find your way back, or worse, get caught and be thrown in the drunk tank."

"Well, what's the worst they can do to us if we are caught? Send us to Vietnam?" Robbie asked, laughing at the irony of the situation.

Reasoning that if they were going to war, they were entitled to spend their last nights of peace enjoying themselves, that evening Dan and Robbie waited for darkness to arrive, and then made their way to the area of the base perimeter about which they had been told. Nearing the fence, they noticed a number of soldiers milling around, and as they got closer, they realized the assembled group was actually a poorly organized line.

"Hey, buddy, what's this line for?" Robbie whispered to the person who was apparently the last in line.

"This is the line to get over the fence," he replied, motioning to the other twenty or so people waiting in front of him. "You can only get over one at a time because there is only so much space where the razor wire is missing."

"Hey, Robbie, everyone on the base must know about this," Dan chuckled.

Their hopes for a quick escape dashed, the two of them patiently waited their turn to climb the fifteen feet of chain link fence. Once over, they spent the night drinking at one of the local bars and flirting with women. When their money was gone, entry back onto the base was gained by negotiating the same stretch of fence they had scaled earlier in the evening. Two nights later, after their third and final night out on the town, Dan and Robbie climbed over the fence one last time, hung-over, broke, but satisfied that they achieved their objective of having some fun before departing for Vietnam.

Chapter 4

-November/December 1967-

"I don't like to kill the tigers, but they eat my peasants."
-Madame Bordeauducq, coffee farmer living in Khe Sanh

In 1967, the communist North was launching violent attacks against the army and civilians of South Vietnam in an attempt to gain control of the country. The United States had come to the aid of the South to prevent the North from accomplishing its goal, which many feared would have caused a domino effect, leading to the spread of communism throughout Asia and perhaps the world. Now, what had started as a small military intervention on the part of the United States had escalated to full-scale warfare.

In January 1967, 30,000 American and Army of the Republic of Vietnam (ARVN) troops fought the Viet Cong, the southern communist forces fighting alongside the North Vietnamese Army (NVA), for three weeks near the Cambodian border in an area nicknamed "The Iron Triangle."[1] During subsequent battles at Dak To, 1,400 North Vietnamese soldiers were killed in savage fighting. As the year progressed, US planes intensified their daily bombings of the North's infiltration route into the South, which had become known as the Ho Chi Minh trail.[2] At Con Thien, American Marines and the NVA slugged it out for four days in September as the North attempted to gain strategic ground overlooking principal routes into South Vietnam.[3] The gruesome body count totals of American, South Vietnamese, North Vietnamese, and Viet Cong soldiers continued to grow, and President Lyndon Johnson raised the American troop ceiling to 525,000.[4]

As the pace and magnitude of the war intensified in the South, the enemy was countering the American troop buildup. Along the 17th parallel (the border between North and South Vietnam) and in the demilitarized zone (DMZ) just below the 17th parallel, the North Vietnamese were amassing thousands of troops for an all-out offensive. The

NVA's plan was simple. They would sweep south from the DMZ and east from Laos to National Route 9. That route was a major access road that ran east to west fifteen miles south of the DMZ, and the only means of vehicular transportation within the region. Having captured Route 9, the NVA would seize the city of Dong Ha, located along Route 9, and continue east to Route 1. They would then move south along Route 1 into Quang Tri City, then through Hue, and finally into Phu Bai. The operation represented a strategically planned avenue of infiltration that, if successful, would win the war for the North.

A major obstacle to the NVA's successful capture of Route 9 was the presence of a United States Marine combat base to the northwest of the village of Khe Sanh. The oblong-shaped base, about a mile in length and a half-mile in width, ran east to west across the Khe Sanh plateau. The plateau itself was an isolated finger of red clay surrounded on all sides by higher mountainous terrain that reached up to 8,000 feet in altitude.[5]

Tucked into the northwest corner of Quang Tri province, roughly ten miles to the east of Laos and fifteen miles south of the DMZ, the Khe Sanh area was critical to the North's ability to smuggle supplies and soldiers into the South.[6] Perched within the Annamite mountain range, the hill-studded area provided exceptional camouflage from observation. A thick jungle canopy hid NVA trails from aerial observation, and dense elephant grass and bamboo thickets made ground observation equally difficult. In addition, the area provided the NVA with five means of approach to Route 9. Khe Sanh Combat Base was placed strategically so that these approaches—the Rao Quan river valley, Hills 881, 861, and 1015, and Route 9 itself—either went through or ran parallel to the base.[7]

American armed forces initiated patrols in the Khe Sanh area in 1962, but not until 1966, when they placed an airstrip on the plateau, was it considered a region of significant military operations. US forces continued to patrol the area through early 1967, but made no major contact with North Vietnamese troops until late April and early May of that year, when units of the 3rd Marine Division became engaged in fierce fighting in the nearby hills. During what became known as the "hill fights," the 3rd Marines gained control of Hills 881 North and South, and Hill 861. On May 11, the 1st Battalion of the 26th Marine

Regiment relieved the previously assigned units of the 3rd Marines and took over operational control of the Khe Sanh Combat Base and the surrounding hills.[8]

On November 1, 1967, the 26th Marines commenced Operation Scotland I.[9] The objectives of Operation Scotland were basically to conduct patrols and reconnaissance missions in order to deny enemy access and provide security within the tactical area of responsibility of Khe Sanh Combat Base and the surrounding hills.[10]

1/26 Marines Command Chronology

In November 197 Marine enlisted joined for duty. During the month, 201 enlisted personnel received a three-day orientation and training program prior to being assigned duty.

November 15, 1967

Dear Mom,

Today I arrived in Da Nang, Vietnam, halfway around the world from Philadelphia. It's so hot here that I stepped off the plane onto the runway and immediately began sweating. Within minutes, my uniform was soaking wet. It was hard to complain about the heat and humidity, though, because at least no one was shooting at me. Vietnam is at war, after all, and I fully expected to get off the plane running and ducking for cover from small arms fire and mortars. I'd imagined chaos and ferocious fighting, like I've seen in movies about D-Day at Normandy, and I was pleasantly surprised to find Vietnam nothing like that at all. An obvious military presence existed, but otherwise, life went on pretty much as normal.

Once on the tarmac, we were separated into divisions and then trucked off to our divisional headquarters to receive regimental assignments. Robbie and I were both assigned to the 26th Marine Regiment, and tomorrow we fly again, this time to Phu Bai, which is the location of the 26th Regiment headquarters. After that, I have no idea, but I'll keep writing to let you know where I am and how I'm doing.

Love,
Daniel

November 17, 1967
Journal Entry

Well, I have my new permanent mailing address. It's a place called Khe Sanh, a Marine combat base tucked into the upper left-hand corner of South Vietnam. In Phu Bai, I was assigned to the 1st Battalion of the 26th Marines, and being as how 1/26 headquarters are in Khe Sanh, here I am.

We flew in yesterday from Phu Bai on helicopters, and disembarking from the chopper reminded me of how I felt arriving in Da Nang. If you can picture it, here I was getting off a perfectly safe helicopter, stepping out into the wide-open backcountry of Vietnam, with no weapons to speak of and nowhere to hide if someone started shooting at me. The combat base is in a valley surrounded on all sides by hills, and as I was leaving the landing zone, all I could focus on was the image of a VC sniper sitting up on one of the hilltops, centering me between his sights. It was really scary. But just like in Da Nang, I got worked up over nothing, since there's absolutely no fighting occurring at the base.

Some more good news is that Robbie was also assigned to 1/26. The chances of us still being together must have been like a million to one. We'll probably be split up into different units sometime soon, but we should still be able to hang out with each other on base, which is cool. And I have to admit, it really helps having a friend around right now.

At the moment, we're being put through a three-day indoctrination course, being taught the "Do's and Don'ts" of being in Vietnam. We're learning about how to act in order to avoid offending the natives and other stuff about local customs. Otherwise, I'm just trying to get adjusted to my new surroundings. It's nothing at all like Philly here, or, I would imagine, any other part of America for that matter. Khe Sanh sure is a long way from home.

November 18, 1967

"Damn, Danny, that was a good meal," Robbie exclaimed, rubbing that portion of his green military issued tee shirt covering his tummy. The two friends strolled across the airfield from a mess hall, each with stomachs full of chicken and mashed potatoes. Although truth be told, the food was less than stellar, but it had been a while since either was fed a home-cooked meal, and they would take whatever freshly prepared food they could get.

"So, what do you want to do tonight?" Dan asked.

"Not sure. What movie is playing?"

"I don't know. We should find out and—" Dan stopped in midsentence. He grabbed Robbie by the arm, interrupting his forward motion. "Hey, Robbie —"

"Yeah?"

"Do you hear something?"

Robbie stood motionless and concentrated on listening.

"Sounds like choppers," he responded, his ear cocked to the sky.

The two looked in the direction of the base's northern perimeter, and sure enough, three helicopters were flying over the surrounding hills, en route to the base. Dan and Robbie sensed immediately that something was wrong, and seconds after the choppers were in sight, dozens of Marines and medics started running from every direction toward the landing zone.

"Hey, Danny," Robbie asked, "What do you suppose this is about?"

November 18, 1967
Journal Entry

. . . Robbie was about to have his answer. A few seconds later, the choppers set down fifty yards from where the two of us stood, the wind from the propeller blades whipping up dirt and debris across the landing zone, momentarily blinding us. Unsure of how to respond, we just watched, trying to figure out what was happening and why everyone was acting so frantically. As we stood there, an officer ran past us, and as he passed, he turned back in our direction and snarled in anger.

"Don't just stand there!" he screamed over the roar of the helicopters. "Get the fuck over here and help with these wounded Marines."

Robbie and I didn't even pause to consider the gravity of what he had just said. Instantly, we began to run, following him toward one of the idling choppers. As I got closer, and some of the Marines gathered near the cabin door started moving out of the way, I could see wounded soldiers on stretchers being unloaded from the chopper. I reached the copter and immediately grabbed one end of the first stretcher off-loaded.

The corpsman on the helicopter pad shouted at me, "Charlie Med. Now! Go!"

A second Marine grabbed the other end of the stretcher, and together we began running awkwardly in the direction of the Charlie Med barracks, the base field hospital located several hundred feet away. As we ran, I couldn't help but look down at the stretcher. On it laid a fellow Marine, badly wounded. He couldn't have been much older than I. He had blue eyes and flowing, bright blond hair, much of which had been soaked red with blood. I'll never forget his face, covered with black dots that resembled little pieces of metal-like gravel. It almost appeared as if someone had poured coarse black pepper all over his face. One arm hung limp off the stretcher, and the other arm, at least what remained of it, was folded across his waist.

As we ran, my eyes froze on this kid's face. I stared into his eyes and realized then that a doctor wasn't going to be of any help. It was the first dead person I'd ever seen. At that moment, my legs turned to jelly, and the rest of my body went numb. I tripped and fell, losing my grip on the stretcher, and watched in horror as the limp, pale, bloody body I was carrying flopped to the ground. Visibly angry at my clumsiness, the Marine carrying the front end of the stretcher began to yell at me.

"Get up, man. Come on. This guy's gonna die if we don't move! Get the fuck up!"

I was scared shitless. My hands were shaking, and I wanted to vomit. I somehow managed to pick myself up off the ground, helped lift the body back onto the stretcher, and carried my end the remaining distance to Charlie Med without falling again. Just as I had figured, though, our efforts had been in vain. I stood there, fixated on the blond hair, blood, and dots of black powder covering the face, and watched a doctor spend ten seconds checking for a pulse before moving to the next stretcher.

—

"Hey, Danny, did you hear me? I asked if you're all right."

Dan, jolted out of his own thoughts, turned and saw Robbie standing a few feet away. He had a dark red blood smear across the front of his uniform.

"Sorry, Robbie. I must have zoned out. What did you say?"

"I said, are you all right? I mean, that was somethin' else just then."

"Yeah, I'm fine. It was a little crazy out there, that's all. I guess I wasn't expecting it."

"No shit. It kinda freaked me out, too."

"Hey, Robbie, man?"

"Yeah, Dan?"

"This shit's for real, isn't it? Some of those guys who were carried off the choppers were dead. I mean, this isn't a game, is it?"

"Naw, man. It isn't a game. This is for real."

November 19, 1967
Journal Entry

Robbie and I stayed up late last night, smoking cigarettes and trying to avoid talking about what had happened. My own thoughts kept returning to that night in California when we watched the movie containing the combat footage. In particular, I kept replaying in my mind the one scene where that soldier was shot dead. I remembered how, at the time, I never thought something like that could happen to me. Now I realize that it can, and it will if I'm not careful. I made a promise to myself last night that I won't let it happen to me, that no matter what, I am going to make it home alive, and I'm intending to do everything I can to keep that promise.

November 20, 1967
Journal Entry

I have to admit, I'm a little anxious about being in Vietnam right now. Honestly, though, I think I have a right to be. Here I am, barely eighteen years old, and I've been thrown smack-dab into the middle of a fucking war. I'm about to be waist high in rice paddies with a rifle and a license to kill, and it doesn't seem to me like a job that should be given to a teenager.

I guess I'm growing up faster than I realized. A couple of months ago, I was going to my prom, buying my first car, and playing ball at the rec center. Now, my tux has been replaced with a flak jacket, my car keys with an M-16, and playing sports with carrying wounded or dead Marines on stretchers.

But I still believe I'm way too young, at least for this, anyway. It's really scary if you stop to think about it. Eighteen-year-olds shouldn't be headed into war. At my age, you aren't even finished growing up yet. But what am I going to do? I can't get out of this now. I'm going to have to be strong, grow up, and become a man fast if I want to survive.

—

The three-day orientation period at Khe Sanh ended, following which Dan was issued his gear, the most important item being his weapon, an M-16 rifle. He also received five magazines, a bayonet, a helmet, and flak jacket. He was then assigned to Charlie Company, 2nd Platoon, 2nd Squad. Amazingly, so too was Robbie Cassidy. Having become best friends subsequent to their first meeting almost three months earlier at advanced training, and despite having drastically different upbringings, they now lived together as companions in the same foxhole in Vietnam. Had they been separated at any time during the three months prior to arriving at Khe Sanh, they more than likely would have never seen or spoken to one another again. But as fate would have it, their friendship would continue to grow and strengthen through the conflict that was the Vietnam War.

November 25, 1967
Dear Mike,
Turns out I joined the beloved Marine Corps to stir shit. You see, there's no in-ground plumbing here in the middle of the jungle, so we have to go to the bathroom in an outhouse. Here, that means nothing more than a tin shack with an oil drum inside that's been cut in half to function as the toilet. Unfortunately, after we're done relieving ourselves, there's nowhere to actually dump all the shit and piss that collects in the oil drum. The only way to get rid of all the waste is to burn it. Since Robbie and I are the two newest guys in our unit, we get assigned the responsibility of stirring all the shit while it burns. I can't even begin to describe to you how bad the smell is. It's horrible. I mean, it's the most disgusting odor I have ever experienced. I can only imagine that even burning flesh doesn't smell that bad. It's all I can do to keep from getting sick. The worst part is that this stuff burns so slowly, and we just have to stand there with these long poles and stir. The good news is that as soon as the next "new guys" show up, we get moved off this duty to something a little more bearable, like filling sandbags. . . .
Take care,
Danny

If not for having to burn human waste, Dan might have actually liked serving in Vietnam. As much as he was concerned about living in a war zone, he perceived Khe Sanh as a sort of lost paradise, somewhat cut off from direct contact with the war being waged in the not too distant countryside. It was full of lush tropical surroundings and beautifully serene green landscapes of dense jungle foliage, thick underbrush, and elephant grass that reached ten to fifteen feet in height. The area, rich in vegetation, produced tropical fruits, rice, and tobacco, and lay claim to one of the largest and most productive coffee plantations in Southeast Asia.[11] Sparkling fresh water streams wound their way down from the mountains, filled to the brim with monster trout. Wild animals, such as boars, tigers, and elephants, roamed through the thickets of the landscape.[12] Rock apes, furry little gray primates that scampered from tree to tree, played with the Marines' minds by throwing rocks at them as they patrolled the jungle (many times these playful yet bothersome creatures would be found strewn across the jungle floor, having been mistaken for enemy soldiers). Rare panthers were even rumored to roam the area around the base.[13] On most days, cloudless skies revealed the most beautiful shade of blue Dan had ever seen, the sun shining brightly overhead.

For the Marines of 1/26, Khe Sanh was their home, and they reveled in their surroundings. They passed their free time by playing basketball or volleyball, or swimming in the nearby streams. At night, after eating an often-delicious hot meal in a mess hall, Marines watched movies at the base theater and drank at the beer hall or, if of sufficient rank, at the officers' club. The soldiers then retired to sleep in their plush tents and bunkers, which were wired with electricity. Relatively speaking, the Marines at Khe Sanh were living the good life. But unknown to those who lived on the base, much of this was about to radically change.

<u>1/26 Marines Command Chronology</u>
```
    December - It appears that the enemy is tak-
ing pains to avoid contact unless entry is made
against infiltration routes or base camp areas.
Increasing number of bunkers, fighting holes,
and trenches give credence to the belief that
```

the enemy is currently marking time around Khe
Sanh Combat Base and preparing for future large
scale operations.
```

## December 2, 1967
**Journal Entry**

    The situation at Khe Sanh has been real quiet for the most part since I arrived. Almost boring. There have been a couple of incidents outside the base where we've seen the aftereffects or heard stories second-hand, but stuffing sandbags, carrying timber, and unloading cargo are generally the order of the day. More recently, however, rumors about an escalation in fighting around the base are beginning to circulate. The grapevine is really active, and there are stories almost daily of an NVA build-up and about discoveries of bunkers and tunnels outside the base perimeter. Just this morning, I was talking to Fallon, from Alpha Company, who said his unit came across something suspicious, fresh digging or something like that, while out on a patrol. He said it looked like the beginnings of a massive trench or bunker system.

## December 6, 1967

    "Okay, guys, listen up. We're saddling up and moving out in five. Make sure you double-check all your gear, because we're not coming back if someone forgets his lucky rabbit's foot. Be ready. Make sure you have enough ammo, and for God's sake make sure you have your canteen filled. It's gonna be hotter than hell in the jungle this afternoon."

    At twenty-one years young, Eli Hanks, who served as the patrol's fire-team leader, weighed in as both the oldest and most experienced of all the Marines heading out on today's reconnaissance mission. Accordingly, when he spoke, Dan listened. Sensing the serious tone in his voice, Dan tightly laced his boots, threw on his flak jacket, and grabbed his M-16 off his cot, triple checking that he had enough ammunition.

    It was early, around 0600 hours, and as was usual for this time of the morning, the fog still hung thick at Khe Sanh. The squad gathered outside, smoking cigarettes and gazing out past the base perimeter toward the jungle while they contemplated what today's patrol had in store for them. Dan glanced around. Aside from Hanks and himself, he counted five others. They included Jake Tatum, a huge hulk of a Ma-
```

rine, who at just twenty was Dan's squad leader, due to his time in-country. J.R. Garcia, Chief, John Abbey, and Robbie rounded out the patrol.

Once everyone was assembled, the squad formed up and made the short trek to the wire. They snaked their way through the maze of the wire to the perimeter, and then disappeared into the tree line. About ten yards into the jungle, Hanks, who was walking point, threw a fist into the air—the sign for everyone to stop moving, get down, and keep quiet.

"Sullivan," Hanks whispered back through the line. "Up front."

Dan moved forward, staying as hunched over as he could.

"Yes, sir?" Dan asked, his voice trembling nervously.

"Okay, first of all, don't 'sir' me," Hanks impatiently scolded. "I'm enlisted, just like you, remember? Second, relax. I know you're nervous. I know this is your first time in the bush, but you have to stay cool. Okay?"

"Yeah. Okay. Sorry."

"Good. Now, listen," Hanks said, handing Dan a long, sharp machete. "I want you to take this and stay close behind me. If I need you to cut me a path, I'll point where to cut, and you do it. Understand?"

Dan nodded. With that, Hanks motioned the group back to its feet, and the patrol once again moved forward, penetrating deeper into the jungle. The squad spent the rest of the morning tiptoeing through the tangled growth, sweeping the area, looking for any sign of the NVA.

After a few hours, the patrol began to circle back to base. At one point, Dan stepped through a clearing and, as he did, spotted something out of the corner of his eye.

"Shit," Dan whispered to himself, dropping to his knee, leveling his sights, and clicking off his safety. His heart was racing, and his throat had gone dry.

"Dan, stop!" Jake Tatum yelled anxiously from behind, quickly reaching to grab Dan's rifle barrel and push it toward the ground. Two hundred yards away, in the direction where Dan had aimed, were two Vietnamese peasants tending the land. "Those are the good guys," Tatum blurted, sounding exasperated. Once it was clear the Marines were not in danger, he explained further. "They're just local Bru farmers. They're totally harmless."

"Sorry, Jake, man. I just thought—"

"Yeah. I know what you thought. It's not your fault. See, that's the great thing about this war. You can't tell the good guys from the bad guys. Don't worry about it. Come on, let's get out of here and go have some beers."

—

Later that afternoon, back from patrol, Dan and Robbie raced to a mess hall for a late lunch.

"Robbie, man," Dan said between bites of food, "that sucked."

"What's that, Dan?"

"That patrolling shit, that's what. My legs are still killing me, it was hot as hell, and the jungle's so muggy and hot, I swear it must have been a hundred fucking degrees under that canopy. Look at me. I'm still soaked from my own sweat. I look like I just took a shower with all my clothes on. Plus, my damn helmet kept falling over my eyes so I couldn't see anything. For the most part I was so frustrated, I had to resist the urge to slam my helmet to the ground. The only reason I didn't was because I was terrified after having been warned about how dangerous it is to take it off in the bush. And with all the noise I was making, it's just a matter of time before Charlie jumps out of nowhere and blows me away."

"Relax, Danny, man. I'm sure we'll get used to it."

"Bro, I can't keep doing that. It was crazy. It was hot, miserable, and it just plain sucked. Sooner or later, if I keep hacking through the bush, I'm gonna get shot."

"Hey, Dan."

"Yeah, Robbie?"

"You gonna eat your pound cake?"

"Damn it, Robbie! Here, have it," Dan exclaimed in frustration as he tossed Robbie his dessert.

December 8, 1967

Dear Mike,

. . . Now our unit spends a lot of time going out on patrol, or setting up ambushes or listening posts at night. Every day, our unit is responsible for one of these three duties. One day we'll do an ambush, the next a patrol, and it seems like I'm on an LP more nights than not.

Setting up an ambush is pretty much what it sounds like. We go out into the bush and set up in a straight line on a position parallel to a trail we suspect Charlie might be using. Once we settle on our position, we place claymore mines and M-60 machine gunners on the ends of the line, and pack everyone else in between the heavy artillery. Then we simply wait for the enemy to approach in front of the position and we open fire. We haven't actually had anyone walk into one of our ambushes yet, but I've been told that when they are sprung, not much gets out alive.

I also mentioned the listening posts, or LPs, which are when we take four or five guys and set up in front of our unit's position at night. Unlike patrols and ambushes, where we are out looking for the enemy, LPs are more of a security measure, kind of like an early warning system to protect against a nighttime attack. The point being, we make sure that Charlie isn't trying to sneak through our lines under the cover of darkness. . . .

Take care,
Danny

December 13, 1967

Dan pulled on his cigarette and looked up at the blanket of stars strung out across the clear night sky. He and Robbie were lying on the roof of their bunker enjoying the cool, refreshing evening breeze. Dan took another drag from his cigarette and, finished with it, flicked it into the trenches.

"You know," he observed as he turned to Robbie, trying to remember far back into his past, "I don't think I have ever seen such a clear sky before, or one with nearly this many stars. It's amazing, really, to think there is so much more out there, so much we don't know about. It kind of puts things into perspective."

"You've gotta be kidding me. You've never seen a sky like this?" Robbie asked in disbelief, ignoring Dan's more existential comments.

"Really, man. I guess there is just too much civilization back in Philly to be able to see the stars this well."

"Well, you've gotta come to Texas sometime. The sky there is so clear, I swear, you can see to the end of the universe."

"I'll definitely have to come see you in Texas someday. Maybe after we get out of here, I'll come down and visit. You can show me your ranch and your horse, and introduce me to your sister."

Dan shot Robbie a smile at this last comment.

"You're getting kind of sweet on my sister, aren't you? I know she's been writing letters to you, too, so don't deny it. She told me so in one of her letters to me."

"Well, I guess a little. She really looked pretty in that picture you showed me, and she seems really nice from her letters, too. Robbie, look, I know you were the one who suggested I write her, but I still feel awkward about it. I just hope you don't mind, you know, her being your sister and all."

"Dan, like you said—I'm the one who got the two of you writing each other, wasn't I? Besides, man, you're my best friend. I'd much rather her be with you than some jerk who's going to treat her wrong."

"Well, just know that means a lot to me."

The two friends sat on the bunker roof for several more minutes, the silence passing between them. Dan stared at the sky and allowed his thoughts to consume him.

"What do you want to do with your life, Robbie?" Dan asked, finally breaking the silence. "I mean, when you get out of this place."

"What do I want to do? I wanna be a hero. I wanna be a hero and win myself a medal, just like my daddy. My daddy got himself a medal, and everyone who knows him says he's a hero. That's it. That's what I wanna do. I mean, at least that's all I have planned for myself so far."

"Well, how the hell are you planning to become a hero?"

"By being in this war and doing something heroic, I guess."

"Shoot, Robbie, we're not heroes. We're just poor, stupid kids. Man, what we're doing is the farthest thing from heroic." Dan paused as he lit up another cigarette. "You know, when you really think about it," Dan continued, "there's nothing heroic at all about war. I mean, maybe we're heroic for not running away to Canada, but war itself isn't heroic. Really, it seems more a matter of survival and watching out for your friends' backs."

"Well, I've never thought of it that way, but still, whether it's heroic or not, I wanna win that medal and make my daddy proud. Speaking of which, did I tell you about the time . . . ."

And as Robbie started spinning more of his entertaining stories about life back in Texas, Dan took another drag from his cigarette and gazed off into the stars.

—

Rumors were now rampantly circulating that the NVA had begun to increase its forces in the area, and that an NVA build-up directly around the base was imminent. These rumors were reinforced by increasing signs of the NVA infiltrating the Khe Sanh area, and it soon became routine for each company to send a small squad or platoon-sized patrol off the base each day to conduct reconnaissance or search-and-destroy missions. The Marines of 1/26 dreaded these patrols, and not just because they involved long, strenuous hikes with heavy packs. There was also the fetid water, blazing hot sun, voracious insects, and razor-edged elephant grass with which to contend. No less daunting was the constant threat of being shot.

Along with conducting patrols and setting up ambushes, listening posts were now a necessity and established every night at dusk by each platoon on base. Each LP consisted of four or five Marines who would set up in front of their unit's position and remain there until dawn to provide security and monitor any likely avenue of approach.[14]

The design of Khe Sanh Combat Base was such that the base was built around a center point, much as spokes of a wheel are centered on a hub. The Marines referred to this center area as Tent City, a hodge-podge of tents where the Marines lived and spent much of their time. Within Tent City was located the 1/26 command post, Charlie Med, the air control tower, the main ammunition dump, and the fuel dispensary. The base runway originated in this center area and extended east to the base perimeter. Moving outwards from the base center, a series of trenches and bunkers encircled Tent City. Next, an elaborate series of defenses, known as "the wire," encircled the trench system. The wire, which formed the base perimeter, and at places was as wide as one hundred feet, was comprised of row upon row of land mines, claymore mines, concertina barbed wire, and ankle-high barbed wire, and was designed to make it impossible for the NVA to penetrate the base.

In order for the Marines to pass through the maze of the wire without killing or injuring themselves, a covertly marked trail from each unit's position provided safe passage. The trail began at a gate through which the Marines entered the wire, and once inside, a zigzag, winding path of engineer's sticks, which were essentially nondescript metal rods, marked the way. Trying to navigate through the wire without knowing this path could prove deadly. But for anyone familiar with the trail, it was relatively easy.

December 18, 1967

At around 2300 hours, the evening's listening post for 2nd Platoon, Charlie Company, 1/26, started its trek out through the wire. Tatum walked point, followed by Dan and Robbie, with Chief and Hayduke bringing up the rear. Tatum slowly led the LP forward, stopping for a moment when they had almost reached the edge of the wire so that he could survey the field of view in front of him. A moment later, he motioned the LP to continue moving ahead.

The night was calm and dark, with the moon playing peek-a-boo behind a group of clouds. The elephant grass gently swayed in the breeze. Unseen insects, animals, and birds chirped, croaked, and buzzed into the darkness. A water buffalo bellowed in the distance.

None of the Marines paid much attention to any of this, however, their eyes and focus intently trained straight ahead into the jungle. Dan was having trouble seeing past the end of his gun barrel through the thick blackness, let alone being able to see what might lie a hundred feet in front of him, and prayed silently that they were not heading in the direction of peril.

Had it not been for the blinding darkness, Dan would have observed the end of the field of coiled concertina wire and land mines only several yards in front of them. And if not for the same darkness, he would have likely also spotted the NVA ambush, dug in just beyond the wire, long before it opened fire.

—

The gunshots exploded, ripping through the silence of the night. Bright, loud, violent flashes of fire streaked overhead.

"Down! Down! Get down!" Tatum hollered at the LP as he grabbed Dan by the arm and pulled him onto the ground. Someone else reached for the radio and screamed into it. "Ambush! There's a fucking ambush out here! We're pinned down! Help us get the fuck out of here before we're all dead!"

Dan's stomach jumped into his throat as he pushed his body as close to the ground as he could. There was little cover and virtually no place to hide, so the best the LP could do was lie prone on the ground and hope the enemy shot high. Rounds were flying everywhere, cracking right past their ears. Green tracers darted overhead. Some shots were so close that Dan could hear them hitting the ground and feel the dirt they kicked up pelting his face. The other Marines around him blindly returned fire, emptying their magazines into the night.

It was the first time Dan was ever the target of gunshots, and he was so overcome with fear that he involuntarily soiled his pants. He was frozen in place, his stomach tied in knots, and his heart was washed over with waves of terror. Even with all the hours of training on the firing range, and weapons drills and practices, nothing could have prepared him for actually being on the other end of the exchange of shots.

On top of the NVA shooting at the LP and the LP returning fire, Marines situated on the base became involved in the firefight, adding to the chaos. Unseen Marines back on the other side of the wire began firing mortars and a battery of quad 50s—four .50 caliber tank-mounted machine guns—over the heads of the LP into the area from where the enemy gunfire was coming. Suddenly, Tatum started screaming again.

"Get up. Everyone get up right now, and get back inside the base. We're going back through the wire."

"Dan, go first. I'll cover you," Robbie insisted, jamming a fresh clip into his M-16 and firing off several rounds. Dan had heard both Tatum and Robbie, but still he did not move. He couldn't. Fear had so overwhelmed all his bodily reflexes that he simply was incapable of forcing himself to get up and run.

"Sullivan! Move!" Tatum hollered in a stern tone. Looking Dan straight in the eyes, he yelled again. "Get the hell up. Move right now or you die right here."

Without even waiting for a response, Tatum pulled Dan off the ground just as quickly as he had pulled him down onto it moments earlier. He then pushed Dan in the direction of the wire, providing covering fire for him from his M-16 as they beat their retreat. The LP shortly passed back through the wire, and moments later, the shooting stopped.

It had been a horrifying and embarrassing experience for Dan. Once he settled down, he changed out of his soiled pants and threw them into the nearest dumpster. Compounding the embarrassment was his realization that while everyone else had gone through several magazines of ammunition, he had been too frightened to fire even a single round. Later that evening, Tatum pulled Dan aside.

"Danny, listen to me very carefully because what I'm going to tell you may save your life. Next time we get into something like that, you can't hesitate for one second. If someone opens fire on you, you return fire. If I tell you to move your ass, you do it as quickly as possible. If you don't, next time you might be dead."

Dan nodded in understanding, and Tatum turned and marched away. Dan put a cigarette to his lips, and as he looked down to light it, he noticed that his hands were shaking uncontrollably.

—

By late December, it was evident that enemy activity around Khe Sanh had increased significantly. The engineers who had designed the trails through the wire had gone to great lengths to conceal the presence of their handiwork, and supposedly, only the Marines at Khe Sanh knew the course taken by each path. However, it did not take a gaggle of generals to comprehend that if the NVA had watched the Marines come and go through the wire so often that they too were familiar with the location of the trails, the NVA must also be aware of many of the other elements of the base's defenses.

Military intelligence now fully believed that the NVA was amassing a large troop contingent around the Khe Sanh Combat Base in preparation for a full-scale attack. On December 13, at the urging of Lt. General Robert Cushman, commander of all the Marines in Vietnam, the 3/26 Marines arrived at Khe Sanh as additional reinforcements.[15] On December 21, 3/26 conducted a five-day sweep of the area northwest of the base, from Hill 881 South to the west toward Hill 918 and back to Hill 689. No contact was made with enemy forces, but 3/26 turned up numerous signs of recent enemy activity.[16]

1/26 After Action Report

```
     December 24 - At 2000H third platoon C Com-
pany  on  Hill  950  received  four  bursts  of
automatic  fire  and  approx.  15  grenades.  Fire
was  returned.  Third  platoon  C  Company  received
five non-serious WIA.
```

1/26 After Action Report

```
     December 29 - At 1125H two squads from Co. B
discovered  four  NVA  at  a  stream  at  XD  803495.
```

Small arms fire was exchanged resulting in two friendly WIA (non-serious). At 1830H three personnel from Co. D fired upon two NVA who came out of the brush in front of their position. Small arms fire was exchanged resulting in two friendly WIA. The NVA were believed to be wounded.

1/26 After Action Report

December 30 - Co. B squad while searching trail at XD 799488 discovered 1 NVA on flank of trail. NVA was engaged and killed.

♠

Chapter 5

-January 1968,
Part 1: The Calm Before the Storm-

"Come out, come out, wherever you are."
-Robert De Niro as Max Cady in "Cape Fear"

January 1, 1968

Dear Mom,
 Merry Christmas and Happy New Year to everyone! I know it's the holiday season back in Philly, but here in Vietnam, you would never be able to tell. There's no mistletoe, no Christmas lights on the trees, and definitely no snow. Christmas and New Years just aren't the same in the jungle. Anyway, in spite of the festive holiday season being upon us, the situation at Khe Sanh is beginning to get a little tense. There are continuing rumors circulating that the NVA is beginning to build up its forces around the base. I personally haven't seen much evidence of this, but other patrols have been coming under fire or across telltale signs of enemy activity.
 Really, though, it isn't so much what I've heard that makes me believe the rumors are true, as much as it is this feeling I have in my gut. It's as if I have an instinct about what's happening here, as if I can envision them peering down on us from up in the hills, through binoculars and riflescopes, just waiting to strike. It's kind of a creepy feeling. I know some of this must be upsetting to hear, but please don't worry about me. I'm in a great unit, and if something goes down, we'll be ready. My platoon is made up of a group of guys with a real sense of duty. We all take care of our fellow Marines and look out for one another—especially Robbie and me. The two of us always watch the other's back and make sure the other one stays out of trouble. Well, give my best to everyone, and again, Merry Christmas and Happy New Year.
 Love,
 Daniel

1/26 Marines Command Chronology

```
   During  the  month  of  January  this  battalion
continued  in  its  assigned  mission  of  defending
the  Khe  Sanh  Combat  Base,  maintaining  security
of  Route  9  in  the  assigned  operating  area,
maintaining  a  sparrow  hawk  platoon,  maintaining
1  [company]  as  regimental  reserve  and  conduct-
ing  a  three  company  search  and  destroy
operation  southwest  of  Khe  Sanh  Combat  Base
during  period  8-12  Jan.
```

January 2, 1968

During the days leading up to January 2, Charlie Company 1/26 was sent on a multi-day patrol southwest of the combat base. Their purpose was to sweep the seven-mile area between Khe Sanh and Lang Vei, where the US Army Special Forces camp was located. After returning from patrol, the company was given time off from any major responsibilities. LPs were still sent out each night, but otherwise, the Marines were told they could expect to spend the next few days relaxing on base. That night, after dinner, Dan headed back to his tent.

"Hey, Danny," Robbie called from his cot as Dan walked through the doorway leading into the sleeping quarters. "Come over here."

"Yeah, what's up?" Dan inquired, casually strolling over toward Robbie and pulling on a freshly lit cigarette.

"Look what J.R. has been hiding," Robbie whispered.

As he began to take another drag on his smoke, Dan looked over toward J.R., and catching sight of what J.R. held, almost choked on his cigarette.

"Shit, J.R. Where did you find that?" Dan asked between harsh coughs.

"Like that?" J.R. asked, grinning like a kid with a new toy. In his hands he clutched an unopened bottle of Jim Bean whiskey, a rare commodity on base. "I've been hanging on to this, looking for the right opportunity to share it, and I figure a couple of days of R&R are as fitting an occasion as any. We were waiting for you to get back from dinner before we opened it. Want some?"

"What do you think?" Dan replied, grabbing his canteen cup and thrusting it at J.R. In a place of few luxuries, the bottle of whiskey was like liquid gold. Between Dan, J.R, Robbie, John Abbey, Roland Dean, and Emmett Lawton, it wasn't long before the entire bottle was empty and the whiskey was sitting warm in their stomachs.

—

On the evening of January 2, each unit assigned to the Khe Sanh Combat Base sent out a listening post at dusk. Around 2030 hours, not long after J.R.'s bottle of Jim Bean was consumed, the Lima Company 3/26 LP detected movement in the vicinity of their position, which was not too far from the base wire. In light of recent intelligence reports regarding an NVA build-up around Khe Sanh, tensions were high, and LPs were being instructed to take no chances. As a result, the listening post was soon reinforced with a full squad, raising the total number of men in the LP to thirteen.[1] With additional firepower on hand, the squad leader made the decision to investigate.

Spreading out in a line, the LP started walking through the brush toward where they had first heard the unsettling movement. The darkness had reduced visibility to almost zero, and they were having difficulty just seeing past the end of their weapons. All of a sudden, one of the Marines thought he observed something in front of him and stopped moving. The whole squad reacted similarly, coming to a complete halt. The Marine confronted the darkness with a verbal challenge.

"Who's out there?" he demanded.

There was no response. Again, he challenged the jungle.

"Identify yourself, or we will fire."[2]

Suddenly, the jungle responded, as fifteen AK-47 rounds were fired over the Marines' heads. All thirteen Marines in the LP, each having eighteen rounds in their clips and each with their weapons set on fully automatic, returned fire.[3]

—

Back on the base, Dan and his buddies were in their tent, reveling in their drunkenness. The whiskey had done its job, and everyone was feeling pretty loose and laid-back. When the firefight outside the perimeter erupted, sudden loud bursts of gunfire echoed throughout the base. Even though the action was taking place hundreds of yards away, the noise from 234 rounds being fired simultaneously by the LP resonated loudly enough to fill Dan's tent. Startled and confused, the Marines of Charlie Company hit the floor and started reaching frantically for their weapons. No one knew for sure what was happening, and that scared them as much as the gunfire itself. Was the base being attacked? Was this the first strike in a major NVA offensive? John Abbey, the squad's M-60 gunner, who had just imbibed his fair share of the Jim Bean, grabbed his weapon and staggered to his feet. He had apparently made up his own mind as to the source of the gunfire.

"They're coming to get us. They're coming to get us," he began screaming in a shrill voice. "Come on guys, it's Charlie. He's attacking the base."

Then, in his panic, Abbey aimed his M-60 in the air and pulled the trigger, firing off dozens of rounds through the tent walls. Smoke and the smell of gunpowder quickly filled the quarters. Spent shell casings littered the floor. The other Marines in the tent, who had just begun to pick themselves off the ground after realizing they were not in any immediate danger, again went flying for cover, rolling under cots and behind trunks in an attempt to avoid being shot by the M-60. Fortunately, Chief and Lawton grabbed Abbey and wrestled away his weapon before anyone was hurt.

Dan awoke the next morning with a terrible hangover. As he lay on his cot staring at the tent ceiling, he endeavored to bring the world back into focus, hoping he would soon shake off his headache. Slowly arising out of his slumber, he yawned and stretched his arms outward, interlocking his fingers, and pressing his palms toward the sky. Still looking up, he gazed with nervous wonderment at his hands and arms, which were covered with small specks much brighter than the rest of his skin. After a moment, Dan let out a sigh of relief when he realized the specks on his body were produced by light, and that he had not been inflicted with some exotic jungle rash. However, still uncertain as to the light's origin, Dan sat up, for a second anxiously wondering if the light meant his cot had been moved outside while he slept, as part of some alcohol-induced practical joke.

When he promptly saw that he was on the inside of the familiar green canvas tent, his concern again diminished. He then let his eyes search the tent interior, taking in his surroundings in an attempt to locate the source of the light. After a moment, he smiled and broke into a low laugh. Dan had solved the mystery. His eyes were now better adjusted to the brightness, and he could clearly make out dozens of tiny sunbeams penetrating the roof and walls of the tent through numerous bullet holes. At the same time, he was reminded of Abbey's antics the previous night. As Dan laid down to go back to sleep, he reflected upon how the miniature sunbeams piercing the tent reminded him of stairways to heaven breaking through large storm clouds, and again quietly laughed to himself.

—

The squad from Lima Company 3/26 killed five of the six NVA soldiers who had opened fire on them the night of January 2. The five who were killed were dead before they hit the ground. The sixth had been wounded, but crawled to safety, as was evidenced by a trail of blood leading away from the bodies. The significance of this incident became apparent when the Marines discovered that those killed were not foot soldiers of low-rank, but rather high-ranking officers in the North Vietnamese Army. The fact that the NVA had committed high-level people for such a dangerous reconnaissance mission could mean only one thing—the North had serious plans for Khe Sanh.[4]

January 5, 1968
Dear Mike,
... Later they brought the bodies of the dead NVA back onto the base and lined them up near Graves Registration for everyone to see. It was like a scene out of an old western movie, where the dead bad guys are put on display in front of the jailhouse as a warning to anyone who might consider getting on the wrong side of the law.
Anyway, it seemed like every person on base went to look at the bodies. Some of the guys even brought their cameras, and were taking pictures and posing with the corpses. Like everyone else, I went to see the bodies, too, but once I saw the scene, I didn't stay long. I had no interest in being a part of that. The guys involved in the incident were being congratulated and joking around, and I admit that on some level, it did feel pretty good to be a Marine. But at the same time, I kept thinking that even though those dead soldiers were North Vietnamese, they were still human beings and deserved a better fate.
Take care,
Danny

January 8, 1968
3/26 Marines Command Chronology
...reports seven personnel outside wire. All units notified on alert....

1/26 Marines Command Chronology
Base defenses were put at 100% because of sighting of 7 personnel outside 3/26 wire. Area was checked at first light and footprints were found.

January 14, 1968
1/26 Marines Command Chronology
Increased emphasis was placed on the defense of the Khe Sanh Combat Base as a result of an over-all intelligence buildup in the 26th Marine's area of operations. An additional company was placed in the perimeter to meet the increased enemy threat.

January 15, 1968
Journal Entry
It was supposed to be my turn for a listening post last night, but I managed to get out of the assignment. Earlier in the day, some lieutenant caught this eighteen-year-old sleeping on his watch. As punishment, the lieutenant sent the poor kid out on the LP in my place. When the listening post got out through the wire, the NVA were sitting in wait for them. From back in the tent, I heard the gunshots and knew right away that our guys had walked into an ambush. I found out later that the kid who took my place was hit the second the shooting began, right in the face. Just like that, he was fucking dead. It's possible he never even heard the shot that killed him. He took my spot, probably saving my life, all because he fell asleep on watch and someone wanted to teach him a lesson. In a day or two, his parents will receive a visit from an officer who will give them a story about how their son died heroically protecting the world against communism. I wonder what they'd say if they knew what really happened?

—

In light of the now obvious enemy buildup, the 2/26 Marines were transferred on January 16 from Phu Bai to the Khe Sanh Combat Base, joining the 1/26 and 3/26 Marines. This marked the first time since World War II that the entire 26th Marine Regiment had operated together.[5] Meanwhile, daily activity continued more or less as usual for Dan and his unit. The routine of rotating from patrols to ambushes to LPs remained unchanged. However, fighting intensified on the surrounding hills and outside the base perimeter as the NVA attempted to gain control of strategic ground around the base. The combat left many Marines and NVA wounded or killed, and the victims were being evacuated to the base with greater frequency. For the Marines at Khe Sanh, it was no longer a question of whether the North Vietnamese would attack the base, but when.

January 20, 1968
Dear Mom,
Well, so much for the beautiful blue skies and sunny days at Khe Sanh. It's winter here now, and that means monsoon season is upon us. Khe Sanh is situated at an elevation of 1,500 feet, and because of the altitude, there are times we're right in the middle of the clouds. Instead of bright blue skies, on most days low clouds and mist consume the valley. At night, fog rolls in and does not burn away until the next afternoon. Unfortunately, it disappears only for a few hours and then, as night falls, another batch of thick fog rolls right back in, covering the area. Sometimes the fog is so thick that I'm not able to see past our own wire. It's becoming much colder here, too, and rain has fallen several times within the last few days.

Anyway, this morning, several choppers carrying casualties flew in from the nearby hills. Apparently, India Company 3/26 got into it with the NVA on Hill 881 North. There were a lot of wounded from the fighting, and some of them were brought to the base for medical attention. The atmosphere is getting really tense around here. Today they had us on 50% alert, and we now have to wear our flak jackets and carry our weapons with us at all times. So much for the boring, beautiful Khe Sanh I once knew.

Love,
Daniel

Fishing With Hand Grenades

At 1400 hours on January 20, a Bravo Company fire-team observed a North Vietnamese soldier surrendering at the end of the base runway. He gave himself up waving a white flag in one hand and his AK-47 in the other. While being interrogated by US military intelligence, the soldier, a high-ranking NVA lieutenant, revealed plans concerning an impending attack on Khe Sanh scheduled for the next day.

That night, every platoon on base took the unusual step of sweeping the section of the wire in front of their respective positions to make sure no NVA units were digging in near the edge of the base perimeter in preparation for the assault. Although unsubstantiated rumors had persisted for weeks, official word had now filtered down through the chain of command confirming that the NVA was completing a large buildup of troops around the base. Because of the possibility that an attack on the base might occur in the very near future, all units needed to be on alert and prepared. The Marines were resigned to the likelihood that they would be attacked. Never in their wildest dreams, however, could the Marines at Khe Sanh have imagined what would occur next.

♠

Chapter 6

-January 1968,
Part 2: The Siege Begins-

*"And you will come to a place
where all you feel are loaded
guns in your face."*

-Billy Joel, *"Pressure"*

January 21, 1968
1/26 Marines Command Chronology
`   At 0458 the Khe Sanh Combat Base came under mortar attack.`

It was five in the morning on January 21, and Daniel Sullivan slept soundly on his cot in Khe Sanh, South Vietnam. He was getting his first good night of rest in a while when, without any warning, he was shaken out of his sleep. As the shaking became increasingly more violent with each passing second, panicked screams filtered into Dan's mind.

"Get up, Dan. Come on, man, wake up! Incoming."

Dan sat up slowly and rubbed the sleep out of his eyes. He turned in anger toward the person who had just awakened him, prepared to give him a piece of his mind, but whoever it was had already rushed out of the tent.

"Incoming? What the hell is incoming?" Dan thought to himself.

Yawning, he glanced around the tent and saw everyone frantically pulling on their boots and grabbing their gear and weapons. Dan caught a glimpse out the tent door as a Marine heading outdoors went flying through it, and saw countless others already outside scrambling in every direction. From the quick look he obtained, it did not escape him that every Marine wore his helmet and flak jacket and was carrying his

M-16. Suddenly, a lieutenant stuck his head through the door. His voice shrieked with urgency and authority.

"Let's go. All of you, grab your shit and get in the trenches, now!" he yelled.

A wave of anxiety rushed over Dan as he snapped out of his half-awake state and jumped off his cot. He immediately threw on his pants and slammed his helmet onto his head, grabbed his boots, flak jacket, and rifle, and rushed outside. As he stepped into the early morning mist, the chill air hitting his face and arms, he heard even more officers barking orders.

All of a sudden, the screams were drowned out as his ears caught the sound of a loud, piercing noise directly overhead. It sounded like a jet plane doing a flyover of the base.

"Man, that plane is flying awfully low," Dan whispered under his breath, looking to the sky to see what type of jet it had been.

With his attention focused upward, at the other end of the base a loud explosion resounded, immediately followed by a giant flash of light that lit up the early morning sky. Dan instinctively cringed, jolted by the deafening sound, and shielded himself by turning away from the blast, even though he was in no danger. Seconds later, he looked back over his shoulder toward where the explosion had occurred, and observed a large ball of fire and dark black smoke pluming into the air. He impulsively looked up toward the sky, to where the sound of what he assumed was a plane had come from, and then again panned back to the growing ball of fire. He realized at that moment that his initial assumption about there being a low-flying jet over the base was wrong.

"My God," Dan exclaimed aloud to no one in particular. "They're dropping bombs on us."

Without further hesitation, Dan lowered his head, and with his boots still in hand, sprinted barefooted across the rough clay ground toward the closest stretch of trenches. As he ran, a series of loud explosions ripped through the base as more incoming rounds rained down from all directions. Jumping into a trench and falling to the dirt floor, he huddled close to the ground. Without pausing, he put on his flak jacket and then his boots, which he laced tightly.

Alone, disoriented, and frightened, Dan remained unsure of what exactly was occurring. Hopeful of finding someone who might have some answers, he began crawling through the trench line. He came upon J.R. and Jimmy Doyle, who were nestled against the wall of a trench, also trying to make sense of the situation.

"This is it," Doyle said. "This is the big invasion they've been talking about."

"What the hell are you talking about?" Dan screamed over a rapid succession of deafening explosions.

"This is NVA incoming. Those explosions are artillery and mortar rounds. I think all this might be cover for their ground troops."

J.R. looked anxious, his hands clenched tightly around his M-16. Seconds later, Robbie came flying over the ceiling of the trench, landing hard on the dirt floor. Lying flat on his stomach, he looked up at the other three Marines from underneath his helmet.

"Gettin' kinda ornery out there, ain't it, fellas?" Robbie asked rhetorically. He had surprised Dan with his unexpected entrance, but Dan was glad to see that his friend was safe.

As the four Marines huddled in the trench, they listened to the whistling of incoming rounds and the loud blasts that sounded upon impact with the earth. A round exploded within yards of their position, shaking the ground. Dan flinched and covered his head with his hands. Dirt flew into the trench, pelting his body. There had not been much work done on the trench line up to this juncture, and the top of the trench wall stood only about chest high. Worried the trenches were providing insufficient cover, but not willing to expose themselves in order to move to a safer area, the four Marines remained in their position, unsure of what to do next. Dan wished he were still asleep.

Suddenly, the world exploded. A deafening noise, like a thousand simultaneous bursts of thunder, echoed across the base. Terrified and shocked, the four Marines flinched and rolled over onto their stomachs, again covering their heads with their hands. Dan's gut felt like it was stuck in his throat from fear, and his ears were ringing loudly.

A North Vietnamese artillery round had just made a direct hit on the base's main ammunition dump, which was only a hundred yards or so from their current position. The resulting explosion sounded like a ton of dynamite being detonated, and the earth trembled as if a massive earthquake was ripping through the base. Bunkers caved in, tents collapsed, and trench walls began to crumble. It was the most deafening sound Dan had ever heard, and was the most unbelievably violent feeling he ever experienced.

"Jesus Christ, what was that?"

"I don't know," Robbie responded, "but that must have been the loudest blast I ever heard."

Their initial fears overcome by their curiosity, Robbie, Dan, J.R., and Doyle all stood up and peeked over the edge of the trench wall to see what had just moved the earth. What remained of the ammo dump after the initial blast was now engulfed in an immense ball of fire shooting a hundred feet into the air. Hot walls of flame that glowed orange and red like a Vietnam sunset jumped into the air, warming the Marines' exposed skin, and black clouds of smoke billowed into the sky.

Moments later, small arms fire began to pepper the base. M-16 bursts sounded from within the trenches, and as Dan and the others stood glancing over the trench wall, the light from muzzle flashes could be clearly seen radiating from the weapons of Marines positioned along other segments of the line. Wanting to do something to relieve their feeling of helplessness, Dan and Robbie each emptied a magazine from their rifles, firing indiscriminately into the surrounding jungle. There was little else they could think to do. As they waited, expecting at any moment to spot enemy ground troops approaching their position, they reloaded and occasionally fired their weapons blindly at the NVA they could not see.

Although now more sporadic, the incoming continued, another round crashing onto the base every couple of minutes. After a few hours, the incoming actually began to help calm the Marines' otherwise shattered nerves, because they knew that as long as it persisted, the NVA ground troops would remain at a distance.

Reports of casualties started filtering in, and cries for "doc" echoed through the trenches. Dan's platoon finally managed to organize itself, the Marines splitting into pairs and cramming into foxholes built every hundred feet or so into the walls of the trench line. Dan and Robbie sat together in a foxhole for hours, shielded by rows of sandbags and boards, and when not firing their rifles at the still invisible enemy, they chain smoked cigarettes and listened to the chatter coming over the radio. There were reports of isolated attempts by small groups of NVA soldiers to penetrate the wire, but no major offensive had yet materialized.

As early morning became late morning, the sun started to appear sporadically, but the fog, compliments of the rainy season, still hung thick over the base. The incoming randomly continued, and the problems with which the Marines were dealing mounted.

The fire swallowing up the main ammo dump blazed hotter, and the unused ammunition and spent shell casings stored near the dump began overheating. The fire caused the stored gunpowder to ignite, resulting in gigantic secondary explosions. Launched airborne by these explosions, the stored ammunition became dangerous flying projectiles. Searing bits of razor sharp metal, hot enough to burn through flesh, and traveling fast enough to rip off an appendage, began to fall into the trenches, creating a deadly situation. As if matters could not get any worse, a supply of tear gas canisters was hit by the incoming, and the irritating gas seeped into Charlie Company's position. To escape the effects of the tear gas and avoid the blistering hot debris raining down on the trenches, the Marines moved into bunkers and put on their gas masks.

January 21, 1968
Journal Entry

The tear gas eventually dissipated, and we were finally able to take off our gas masks. Thank God, too, because those things are really claustrophobic. The fire at the dump, however, is still raging out of control. Fire trucks were out there earlier, trying to extinguish it, but with all the exploding ammunition and NVA incoming, battling the fire was just too risky for the firefighters. As for the incoming, it tapered off a little this afternoon, but seems to be building up again. It's not at the level of this morning, but there's enough that we can't free our minds of the threat. Every few minutes, we can hear overhead the jet noise of a rocket, or the incredibly loud locomotive sound of artillery. Then, a second or two later, just like thunder following lightning, a deafening explosion occurs as the round crashes onto the base. As we sit here, guessing what's next, we all become a little more unnerved with each subsequent explosion, wondering whether one of the rounds is eventually going to find us.

1/26 Marines Command Chronology

At 0500 the battalion received approximately 100 82 mm mortar rounds and 20 122mm rockets throughout its assigned sector within the Khe Sanh Combat Base.

—

And thus began the siege of the Khe Sanh Combat Base. Six thousand Marines at Khe Sanh were encircled by what was estimated to be as many as 40,000 NVA troops. Of those 40,000, approximately half the NVA soldiers were believed to be positioned immediately surrounding Khe Sanh, and the other 20,000 within a twenty-mile radius of the base. The man who had personally spearheaded the North Vietnamese troop buildup, and who was presently directing the siege, was North Vietnam's defense minister, Vo Nguyen Giap.[1] Giap was the same commander who engineered the defeat of the French at Dien Bien Phu in 1954 by surrounding them with 40,000 Viet Minh soldiers and shelling them with heavy artillery until successfully overrunning their base.[2] Dien Bien Phu was the decisive battle of the first Indochina war, and with the French defeat, effectively ended that conflict.

At Khe Sanh, Giap's dream of a second Dien Bien Phu began to unfold.[3] The 40,000 soldiers now encircling Khe Sanh composed the largest, most highly concentrated, and best-equipped unit the NVA had ever assembled.[4] By January 21, four NVA divisions encircled the base. To the north was the 325th C Division, to the east the 324th B Division, to the south the 304th Division (the same division that had fought so effectively at Dien Bien Phu), and to the southeast were elements of the 5th Division.[5] In support of their ground troops, the NVA had targeted Khe Sanh with numerous Russian-made 152-mm howitzers, which were located in Laos and north of the demilitarized zone.[6]

—

Throughout the night of January 21 and into the morning of January 22, the incoming continued. Mortars, artillery, and high-powered rockets pounded the base, tearing portions of its surface to shreds, while the whistling and explosive bursts of the rounds sounded overhead. The base shook each time the projectiles impacted its earthen floor, sending smoke, dust, and clay billowing into the air.

Significant damage was now being inflicted upon large parts of the base's infrastructure. Flying shrapnel and debris, which lodged in the flak jackets and exposed flesh of those caught in the open, was wounding Marines throughout Khe Sanh. The medical doctors, or "docs," struggled to keep up with the flow of wounded, bandaging gashes caused by shrapnel, and tending to other serious wounds as quickly as conditions permitted.

For some Marines, medical attention was no longer of help. The blood-soaked bodies of young victims were laid out on the base's red clay, covered by drab olive green ponchos, where they would remain until it was deemed safe enough to carry them to Graves Registration.

January 22, 1968
Dear Mom,
. . . The sound that I had initially thought was a low-flying jet had actually been an NVA rocket. Since then, we have received a constant bombardment of NVA incoming. The intensity of the incoming varies, but it has never completely stopped for more than a couple of minutes since it started. Anyway, I just wanted to let you know that I am still alive, and I'm doing about as well as one can, given the situation. I am thinking of you all to help get me through this. Keep me in your prayers.
Love,
Daniel

January 23, 1968
Journal Entry
Two days later, and the incoming still hasn't stopped. Since it's not safe for us to be in the open anymore, we've had to move everything underground into the trenches. There wasn't much left above ground anyway, since the North Vietnamese have blown the hell out of most of it over the last two days.

Inasmuch as we're now basically living underground, yesterday we went to work improving the trench and bunker system. We spent the morning digging trenches and filling sandbags under the thick cloud cover that has blown in with the monsoons. We withdrew under cover for the rest of the day once the sun burned its way through the fog in the late morning. As night arrived, we went back to work, digging in the dark.

We dug deep into the red clay, working feverishly through hunger, fatigue, and blisters, tunneling until we could stand on the trench floor and look up at the trench ceiling. Then we dug even deeper. Digging the trenches down far enough to avoid shrapnel has now become a matter of life or death. Also, if we don't dig deep enough, we take the risk of having a rocket fly in and tear off our heads.

After working through the night, our trench depth has reached about eight or nine feet. Aside from the added protection it provides against rockets and artillery, the extra height also helps protect us from sniper fire, which has become a huge danger. However, we soon learned that the trenches do not necessarily protect us from mortars.

We found out about this unanticipated problem from a Marine named Zeke, who serves with the 1st Battalion, 9th Marines. Zeke had temporarily been with our unit because when his battalion arrived yesterday at Khe Sanh, there was so much chaos on base they couldn't immediately be designated living quarters. Instead, all the 1/9 Marines were for the time being divided up so that a few of them were assigned to each existing unit's sector. As we dug trenches, Zeke started telling us stories about having served at Con Thien, where the situation had been somewhat similar.

As he helped us shovel dirt into sandbags, he began insisting that no matter how far down we planned to dig our trenches, we needed to take additional precautions to protect ourselves from mortars. Zeke warned us that although mortars are less devastating than artillery and rockets, they are a lot sneakier. He explained, to those of us who weren't familiar, that rockets fly parallel to the ground and will just crash into the trench ceiling. As long as we stay in the trench and keep our heads down, the worst a rocket will do is scare the shit out of us and shower us with dirt. Mortars, however, fly in a high lofting arc, kind of like a baseball pop-up, and have a tendency to land right in the trenches.

To show us how to protect ourselves, Zeke started right at floor level by digging a hole at a ninety-degree angle to the floor down into the side of the trench. Then, after changing direction and carving a couple of feet into the wall, he started digging down again. When he was done, the trench looked something like this:

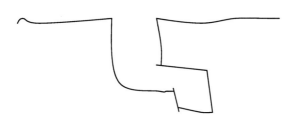

Zeke then showed us how we could roll into the cutout in the wall and drop down into the second hole. It was kind of like a trench within a trench. If we acted quickly enough when we heard incoming mortars, the "mortar pit" would provide us additional protection from any mortar round that flew into our line. The key to a mortar pit working, of course, is that we have to make certain we're listening for the distinctive pop and whistle.

Along with improving the trench system, we went to work reinforcing our bunkers. The bunkers, which were located along the trench lines every hundred yards or so, became critical because they provided us with significant protection from the incoming and were now our full-time living quarters. Robbie and I saw some guys building weak bunkers, not really giving a shit about what they were doing. They would just throw down a layer of steel runway matting and a couple of sandbags to serve as the roof, and figured they were safe. Not our unit, though. We took the time and effort to design our bunker to survive almost anything.

Bunkers are essentially just holes dug into the ground, measuring about ten feet by ten feet, with their roofs built at ground level. Since the roof is the only part of the bunker structure vulnerable to incoming, with the rest of the bunker located underground, like a basement, we concentrated on building our roof to be as strong as possible. We started by laying down railroad ties across the hole in order to provide a foundation for the other components. On top of that foundation, we placed a layer of steel runway matting, then a couple of layers of sandbags, and then another layer of matting. After that, we threw on one more layer of sandbags for good measure. Finally, we added anything else we could find or pilfer that we thought might help stop a rocket or mortar. For example, we grabbed empty shell casings and empty metal ammunition canisters, packed them with dirt, and onto the roof they went. By the time we had assembled all of the materials, our bunker roof probably measured two or three feet thick.

While we're confident all that reinforcement should protect us from a rocket or mortar attack, artillery rounds are a completely different story. There's not really much that can stop one of those bastards. As we are witnessing, artillery will blast through just about anything—even steel and concrete. When it comes to artillery, I guess the best we can do is pray that we never take a direct hit.

January 24, 1968
Journal Entry

Because of the NVA buildup, it is no longer safe for us to run patrols or ambushes off the base. LPs are still sent out at night, but otherwise there is no movement on our part beyond the base perimeter. For that matter, there is not much movement by us at all. The constant danger presented by the incoming leaves us confined, most of the time, to the relative safety of the trenches. In addition to the incoming, another consequence of the enormous North Vietnamese buildup around the base is that we now continually draw sniper fire from NVA soldiers perched in the surrounding trees. There are thousands of NVA soldiers within a 1,000-foot or so radius of the base, and any well-trained sniper with a rifle can easily kill someone from that distance. These snipers make all the shit we are dealing with at Khe Sanh so much worse, and give us even more incentive to stay put in the trenches.

Ironically, the dense, ever-present fog that accompanies the monsoon season, and initially added to our sense of gloom and misery, has turned into our ally. The thick fog that blankets the base provides us cover from the snipers. Just as we can't see off the base, they can't see onto it to sight a target. We've learned, however, that unless there is heavy fog cover, it is a bad idea to emerge from the trenches during daylight hours. To do so means you run a real risk of being shot.

January 25, 1968
Journal Entry

To keep us occupied so we don't go stir-crazy sitting in the trenches all day, this morning we were ordered on a work detail to lay down more tanglefoot in front of our position. We woke up early, while it was still dark, and headed into the wire. Aside from me, the detail included Robbie, Jimmy Doyle, Steinmetz, and Frankie Rodriguez. Even as it began to get lighter out, the fog remained thick enough to provide us plenty of cover, so we felt fairly safe. We were almost finished when, all of a sudden, the fog lifted. Just like that, it was gone in a blink of the eye. Steinmetz was the first to notice. I could immediately tell from the tone in his voice that we were in trouble. He started cursing and screaming that the fog was lifting and we needed to get out of there right away.

As soon as he said something, we started to gather our equipment, but it was already too late. Within seconds, we began to draw sniper fire. Before we even heard the shots, the first few bullets hit the ground around us, harmlessly kicking up dirt. A split second later, we heard the delayed sound of rifle fire, the soft cracks echoing over the valley.

My heart started pounding, and adrenaline coursed through my body. We all turned to beat a retreat, leaving our gear where it was, but as we were doing so, Jimmy caught a couple of rounds in his stomach. He staggered backwards and fell over, and everyone else dove to the ground, seeking protection behind what little cover was available. Badly hurt, Jimmy began to scream and howl as blood seeped between the fingers of his hands, which had instinctively moved to cover the wounds. From my prone position, I watched as Jimmy, still lying on his back, violently pounded his feet against the ground while writhing in pain. I could see blood spreading across his torso, soaking his uniform, and there was a trickle of blood coming out of the corner of his mouth. We all hesitated running to him, aware that the sniper was probably waiting for us to do just that so he could get clear shots at the rest of us.

Knowing we could not leave Jimmy there to die, after the shooting had stopped for a few minutes, we cautiously began crawling on our bellies toward where he was lying. Sure enough, after moving barely a few feet, we started to draw more sniper fire. We pulled back, wondering how to time making another break for him. While we were regrouping, a medical corpsman, who had been watching from the base, took advantage of a lull in the firing and began racing through the wire to join us. The movement of the corpsman attracted several more rounds of fire, but it stopped again once he reached cover, and several minutes later it was the corpsman who was the first to summon up the courage to make a break for Jimmy. For whatever reason, the sniper had now given up on us, and there was no more shooting. Still, not taking any chances, we moved as quickly as we could to join the corpsman and help pull Jimmy behind cover. Once this was accomplished, we remained stationary for several more minutes, trying to stop Jimmy's bleeding, and hoping the sniper was in fact done with us.

Jimmy was passing in and out of consciousness. His screams had quieted to nothing. His skin was turning white, and his body began to shudder as he lost more and more blood. To calm myself, I looked into the jungle and focused on the thousands of trees, in one of which the sniper was possibly hiding. I felt completely useless. In spite of all the chaos, as we sat there I had a few moments to reflect on how quiet it had become. Birds chirped in the distance, and the trees swayed in the breeze. I listened as my heart rhythmically pounded in my chest, and noticed that I was breathing incredibly hard, the crisp air filling and then leaving my lungs.

When we decided we couldn't wait any longer to get Jimmy medical attention, we picked him up and carried him back through the wire as fast as we could. Someone had called ahead for a doc, who was waiting for us when we got into the trench. He took a quick look at Jimmy's wounds and ordered him placed on a chopper. Five minutes later, Robbie and I were each on our second cigarette since reaching the trench.

January 27, 1968

On January 27, the 37th Army of the Republic of Vietnam Ranger Battalion arrived at Khe Sanh, becoming the fifth and final battalion defending the base. They joined the three battalions of the 26th Marines and the 1/9 Marines. The Marines, who had more respect for the NVA than for the ARVN, actually resented their supposed South Vietnamese allies. A primary reason for this attitude was the ARVN practice of leaving their wounded and dead on the field of battle. One of the main tenets of the Marine Corps is that they always recover their wounded and dead, never leaving anyone behind on the battlefield. The Marines viewed the ARVN habit of leaving fallen comrades behind as cowardly, dishonorable, and unbecoming of soldiers. Compounding their disdain for the Vietnamese allies was the opinion held by many of the Marines at Khe Sanh that the only reason ARVN forces had even bothered to show up stemmed from political, not military, considerations. This proved to have been an astute conclusion.

General William Westmoreland, the commander of the US forces in Vietnam, later acknowledged, "To assure ARVN participation in what I deemed to be an important fight, I insisted that the South Vietnamese contribute an ARVN ranger battalion."[7]

ARVN Colonel Hoang Ngoc Lung was even more to the point when he stated, "Not until the fighting had been in full progress did the [Republic of Vietnam] decide to deploy one ARVN ranger battalion to the base, more for political than tactical reasons, evidently."[8] It was no wonder that most Marines viewed the ARVN presence at Khe Sanh with a measure of disgust and contempt.

January 28, 1968
Journal Entry

Only the really brave or really dumb dare to venture out into the open these days. Those who do can be seen sprinting across the base in a low crouch, guarding themselves as best they can from the impending rounds of mortar and sniper fire they are sure to draw. It makes you curious, though, why they would even risk it, since there is nothing above ground at Khe Sanh anymore. Anything of value that hasn't already been blown to hell is buried in the red clay for protection from the constant shelling. Even the trucks at Khe Sanh are underground, parked in inclines bulldozed out of the clay.[9]

Everything about life here at Khe Sanh has changed. Pickup games have ceased, the mess halls have stopped serving meals, and we have moved from fairly comfortable and clean confines to dim and stinking trenches. We do everything in the trenches now. We live, eat, and sleep in them, and to be blunt, life in the trenches sucks. For example, with no mess halls, there are no more hot meals. All we have now are C-rations, the ready-to-eat meals served out of tin cans. Even worse, there is never enough food to satisfy our hunger. With all the problems we're having being re-supplied, we are down to only two meals of C-rats a day. There is a scarcity of drinking water, and forget about water for bathing or shaving. Some guys are starting to smell really funky, and we don't have any clean uniforms into which to change. In fact, most of us are still wearing what we wore the day the siege started. Almost everything else we owned was destroyed or lost.

We can't get out of the trenches at all during the day, because if we do we'll get shot, or rockets and artillery will tear us to pieces. We even have to go to the bathroom in the trenches. There are designated areas every so often in the line where we've dug out holes to be used as toilets, but nothing prevents the stench from blowing through the lines. The trash is piling up, and it is beginning to smell like a landfill down here. It's dirty, there's hardly any light, and the rats are unbelievable. We sit here in the filthiest, most miserable, most God-forsaken strip of land on earth, and all we can do to occupy our time is absorb the daily barrage of rockets, mortars, and artillery.

The hardest thing about all of this is the uncertainty and lack of control over the situation. You never know when your time will arrive to end up in the path of an impending round. What it comes down to is simple luck and fate, which none of us have any power to control. Every time a round lands, it is only those two circumstances—luck and fate—that determine whether the round lands harmlessly in the middle of an open area, or in a trench, possibly ripping someone in half. Besides saying a prayer, all we can do is roll up into tight little balls, let our flak jackets cover us, and hope for the best.

Whenever somebody gets it from incoming, it is not long before word spreads from unit to unit. Even worse, sometimes you find out about the loss of fellow Marines by seeing the dead with your own eyes. Having to look at the pale, lifeless faces may be the worst part of all. Afterwards, I always wonder who's going to get it next. Will it be me? Will it be one of my friends? I keep trying to convince myself that it won't be, because we have dug the deepest holes at Khe Sanh.

January 29, 1968
1/26 Marines Command Chronology
TET cease fire commences at 1800 until January 31 0600.

January 30, 1968

As January ended, the Marines at Khe Sanh were becoming increasingly restless. They had been cooped up in the trenches for nine days, and were tired of having to absorb the incessant incoming without being allowed to make any offensive moves to retaliate.

Separately, a cease-fire was worked out between the North Vietnamese and the Americans for the TET Nguyen Dan festivities, which celebrated the Asian New Year that fell on January 30. American intelligence suspected that the NVA would break the cease-fire and attack in force throughout South Vietnam. Many of the Marines at Khe Sanh also believed the NVA would violate the cease-fire, and that one of the NVA's main targets would be their combat base. After more than a week of not being able to fight back from their positions, the Marines were actually looking forward to being attacked by real-life humans instead of inanimate missiles. The defensive posturing had worn the Marines' patience thin. They were not trained for, nor had they expected, what was now happening, namely not being permitted to take the offensive.

On the night of January 30, as the people of South Vietnam partied in the streets across the country, Viet Cong rebels and NVA soldiers were mixing in among the celebrants. At 0300 hours on the morning of January 31, the enemy struck. 36,000 NVA and Viet Cong troops launched a widespread offensive throughout the entire country.[10] They attacked almost every major city in South Vietnam, including the national capital of Saigon and thirty-six of the forty-four provincial capitals.[11] Fierce fighting in Saigon was capped by an attack on the United States embassy by VC guerrillas. It took US troops hours to reclaim those portions of the embassy that had temporarily fallen into the hands of enemy fighters.[12]

It was during the TET offensive, in the city of Hue, that some of the most ferocious combat of the entire war occurred. The NVA captured Hue and seized the Citadel, the central area of the city and site of the ancient Royal Palace, where they raised the VC flag. Gaining permanent control of Hue would have marked a significant and major victory for the NVA. Hue was the cultural and religious center of Vietnam. Control of the city would have provided a tremendous boost to the North's morale, and would also have helped to create a more favorable public opinion in the South toward the communists. Perhaps more importantly to the Marines at Khe Sanh, Hue lay astride Route 1, the main north-south artery in South Vietnam. Capturing Hue would have afforded the North the ability to block all reinforcements and supplies to troops in the northern part of the country, including Khe Sanh.[13] Appreciating the strategic value of the city, it took US forces an entire month of bloody fighting to reclaim Hue, regaining it block by city block. The prolonged and bitter fighting left scores of American soldiers dead and wounded, and virtually the entire city of Hue structurally destroyed.

While the TET offensive was a failure from a military standpoint, the North losing thousands of men in the process, in many respects the countrywide ground assault proved an incredible success. TET gave the North worldwide standing by demonstrating their will and ability to fight. In the United States, protesters seeking to sway public opinion against the war initiated a major push, buoyed by the large number of casualties suffered by American troops. TET also resulted in a severe dampening of optimism in the US that an allied victory could be achieved.[14]

January 31, 1968
Dear Mom,

I guess you have heard about the TET offensive by now. All night we were receiving continuous reports over the radio about the fighting, but despite the widespread assault, nothing really significant happened here at the base. There was lots of incoming, but that has been going on for a week and a half, so it was nothing new. I know you don't want to hear this, but we were frustrated by reports that everyone except for us was being attacked. We figure let the NVA bring it on, and let's get this over with. Ten days of continuous incoming is more than we can stand.

On another note, want to hear about the brave ARVN whose country we are protecting? They were given leave for the TET holiday so they could visit with their families, and half of them never even returned to their units. Can you believe that? Half of all the ARVN forces went AWOL after TET. They deserted their own country that we are being killed defending.

You want to know what else I discovered? While we have American kids here, eighteen and nineteen years old, fighting for South Vietnam, there are eighteen and nineteen year old South Vietnamese going to college in Saigon. I mean, it's a joke. I can appreciate American kids going to college instead of coming to Vietnam, but you'll never be able to get me to understand how there are South Vietnamese kids of military age who aren't serving in the military. How is that even possible? For God's sake, this is their country! I'm not sure why the ARVN are even in uniform. In my opinion, it's just a weak attempt at creating a sense of solidarity between the US and South Vietnam, which really is all just a lot of crap anyway. I mean, they don't even want us here. I wish we could just pack up everything and go home. . . .

Love,
Daniel

♠

Chapter 7

-The Siege Continues-

"I'd rather be in Philadelphia."

-W.C. Fields

February 1, 1968
1/26 Marines Command Chronology
    Throughout the month of February increased emphasis was directed toward the defense of the Khe Sanh Combat Base. Additional bunkers were constructed and existing bunkers were improved, trench lines were improved and deepened, additional protective wire was emplaced and six mine fields were laid covering the principal avenues of approach into the battalion defensive sectors. Daily wire checks and tunnel searches, using all types of listening devices, were conducted to preclude enemy breaches of the perimeter. During the entire month this battalion received sporadic to intensive rocket, artillery and mortar fire resulting in light to moderate damages to facilities, equipment and injury to personnel.

February 2, 1968
    "Happy birthday to you. Happy birthday to you. Happy birthday, dear Dan. Happy birthday to you."
    "Go ahead, man, blow out the candles and make a wish," Robbie insisted, grinning from ear to ear.
    "Robbie, there aren't any candles," Dan responded, stating the obvious.
    Laughing, Robbie egged Dan on.
    "Well, make a wish anyway, and eat your cake."

Dan smiled, sighed, and took a bite out of his birthday cake.

"Oh, Robbie, man, this is absolutely disgusting," Dan said, grimacing.

To celebrate Dan's birthday, Robbie had taken a pound cake from his C-rations and covered it with a combination of cocoa mix and water, which he was trying to pass off as icing. As Dan chewed, his emotions alternated between wishing he could spit the food out, and trying desperately to keep it all in his mouth, as he laughed at the ridiculousness of Robbie's makeshift birthday cake. While Dan knew that Robbie was trying to be a thoughtful friend, he had mixed feelings about the fact that Robbie had managed to ruin a perfectly good piece of pound cake. Still, despite the cake being horribly soggy and excruciatingly sweet, Dan ate every last bite. Taking into account the circumstances, being given a birthday cake was one of the nicest gestures anyone had ever done for him.

"Happy birthday, Dan."

"Yeah, man, happy birthday."

"Thanks, J.R. Thanks, Frankie."

"So did you get any presents?" Roland asked.

"My mom sent me a card, but that's about it." Dan took a last bite, finishing off the cake. "Hey, guys, thanks again," Dan said with genuine sincerity, as he wiped cocoa off his fingers and onto his shirt. The new muck hardly mattered, as his uniform was already completely covered in filth. Having finished the cake, Dan lit a cigarette and leaned back against the wall of the bunker.

Nineteen years old, he thought. What in the hell was a nineteen-year-old doing in a place like Khe Sanh, anyway? At nineteen, he was only an immature kid. An adolescent. Still just a teenager. Yet here he was, fighting in a savage war, seeing people around him die every day. This war wasn't the place for anyone, but especially not for a kid.

February 3, 1968
Journal Entry

The incoming continues to be a constant threat to our lives. It has reached the point where a device has been installed on the base to warn us of incoming rounds. Supposedly, we have tapped into the North Vietnamese radio system, and when we intercept messages ordering artillery attacks, a loud, piercing siren is blasted across the plateau. Nobody really believed the warnings at first, given that no one thought our intelligence was actually that precise. That was, until the signal started to prove its effectiveness. Now when we hear the siren go off, we get our shit together and hunker down in the trenches.

Basically, we have three different types of incoming to deal with—mortars, rockets, and artillery. Mortars are shot out of long, mobile tubes, and have a relatively short range that makes them ideal for the NVA to fire from positions near the base. There are hundreds of NVA right outside the perimeter who launch mortars at anything they see move. They just drop this little missile into the tube and off it goes. Fortunately, mortars have some inherent weaknesses as a weapon. When a mortar is fired out of the tube, it makes a very distinctive sound, like a "poof," and being that the mortar cannons must be fired from close range, we can actually hear the poof. Additionally, mortars are relatively slow compared to rockets, so at the moment when we hear the poof of a fired mortar, we know we have a few seconds to scramble into our mortar pits.

A rocket, on the other hand, is quick as lightning. We don't hear them when they're launched like we do the mortars, but we always hear them approaching. In my opinion, they sound exactly like a jet. Unlike mortars, though, incoming rockets come in so fast that there isn't much time to react, which is a major reason we stay down in the trenches as much as possible. You should see one of these things. They're long and ugly looking, with propellers on the back, and they screech overhead like a warplane. And man, do they do the job.

Of all we have to contend with, however, the never-ending artillery barrage is worse than even the snipers, hunger, filthy living conditions, and mortars and rockets. We can't hear the artillery fired because it is coming all the way from Laos, but we can definitely hear it barreling through the sky right before it hits. The first time I ever heard an approaching artillery round, it sounded as though a huge locomotive was rolling through the base. The explosion and the resulting hole that it left when it hit were beyond belief. It was so loud and devastating, I truly thought the earth was going to split in two. When the early warning siren goes off, and we hear the impending round churning through the sky toward us, all we can do is duck for cover and pray. There's nothing that can stop artillery, so it doesn't matter how well you built your bunker, or how deep you dug your trench. If you're there when an artillery round hits, you're fucked.

After a long day of incoming, you can walk around here and see bodies being carried off to Graves Registration, with more dead lying on the ground, covered by green ponchos. You can spot guys digging through broken timbers and collapsed oil drums to remove Marines who were buried underneath the rubble after artillery rounds crashed into their bunkers. Not a day goes by without someone dying after catching shrapnel. It's not like the base is literally covered with bodies, but let's just say I'm beginning to get tired of seeing eighteen and nineteen-year-old Marines being zipped up into body bags.

—

It was no coincidence that the initiation of the NVA siege of Khe Sanh coincided with the beginning of Vietnam's monsoon season. Because of the intense winter downpours that now saturated the country, much of Route 9 was impassable. Although the only major access road in the area, Route 9 was for the most part, even under the best of circumstances, nothing more than a narrow strip of dirt. Now, due to the heavy rains, portions were flooded, often causing the roadbed to wash away. The combination of the miserable weather and the NVA overwhelming the area prevented any attempt by military engineers to repair the road, thereby eliminating the possibility of truck convoys reaching Khe Sanh. Consequently, all attempts to re-supply the 6,000 Marines at Khe Sanh by ground were abandoned, at least until the monsoon season ended in late March.

As a result, the only method of providing the besieged Marines with food, water, ammunition, and other supplies during the winter months was through the air. This mammoth task was undertaken by a fleet of American helicopters and transport planes that included UH-34, CH-46, UH-1E, and CH-53 helicopters, and C-123 and C-130 transports.

Re-supplying the base by air proved no simple task. Even without the siege, the regular cloud cover in the valley would have made re-supply by air difficult, if not impossible. Most of the time, the cloud ceiling at Khe Sanh was no more than 100 feet. Accordingly, pilots were forced to feel their planes through the thick cover while coordinating with air traffic control on the base so they could land their aircraft. That the planes were allowed to land at all was due solely to the horrendous condition of Route 9. United States Air Force regulations stipulated a minimum 300-foot ceiling in order for an aircraft to land, and only because ground transport had been cut off was the restriction lifted.[1]

As if the cloud cover did not present the pilots with enough of a challenge in the face of the ongoing siege, re-supply of the base through the air became a deadly game of cat and mouse. Planes and helicopters landing at Khe Sanh were sitting ducks, easy targets for the North Vietnamese mortars. In the early stages of the siege, aircraft landed on the base runway. That practice was brought to a halt, however, once the NVA became proficient at launching barrages of incoming timed to destroy the aircraft and the supplies they carried, and which would wound and kill many aircraft crewmembers.

With that practice abandoned, the Air Force turned to the use of Low Altitude Parachute Extraction Systems (LAPES), or as they were known on the ground, "skid drops." In order to deploy a skid drop, a plane would descend to within ten to twenty feet of the runway without actually landing. The pilot would then release large parachutes that, in turn, pulled large steel pallets covered with cargo out of the rear of the plane. The pallets slid along the runway until the parachutes brought them to a stop. The plane could then quickly gain altitude and safely fly away, without having to spend time sitting on the runway, where it was dangerously exposed to enemy fire. This method of supplying the base worked successfully for a short while, but was terminated when one of the sleighs went out of control and skidded off the runway, crashing into a bunker and killing three Marines.

Finally, the Marines turned to parachute drops as the method for supplying the base. As the name suggests, parachute drops involved dropping bales of supplies onto the runway by parachute. While the safest of all the methods adopted, parachute drops had one major drawback, simply that on occasion the wind would carry the supplies astray, into the jungle and into the hands of the North Vietnamese.

February 5, 1968

Dear Mom,

I expect this will be quite a long letter because I have so much to tell you about. It also doesn't hurt that there's not much to do but sit here and write. Despite the re-supply effort that I described in my last letter, supplies are still difficult to come by around here. Food is scarce, and drinking water is even harder to find. There were a few days recently when we didn't get anything to drink at all. We have a water point out in front of the firebase, not far from where we are positioned, but it cannot be used anymore. The problem is that we can't go down there inasmuch as NVA are lying in wait for us. Because of that danger, the water we do get to drink has to be flown in by plane or helicopter. At the moment, we're limited to a canteen cup a day, which is only about 6 ounces of water. It is hardly enough. Sometimes we're so thirsty we lay out ponchos to catch rain, or even just the morning dew.

We are short on most other supplies, too. Many of us need new flak jackets because those we are wearing are rotted or were torn apart by tiny bits of shrapnel. Our uniforms are ragged and tattered, and reek of mildew and body odor. There are no clean changes of socks, underwear, or tee shirts, and hot meals are a thing of the past. All the food we get now is strictly C-rations. C-rations are these boxed meals that contain a canned entrée, such as beef or ham, a canned vegetable, and a dessert, which hopefully is a pound cake because it's the only edible food they give us. C-rations also include tissue paper, toilet paper, bubble gum, and sometimes cigarettes. It's obviously nothing glamorous, just the fundamentals. Needless to say, C-rations don't satisfy the voracious appetites of growing, teenage Marines. In order for us to get enough to eat, or enough of even the most basic supplies, pilfering has become a necessity.

At night, under the cover of darkness, Robbie and I have on a few occasions snuck over to the landing zone to see if there are pallets of undistributed supplies lying around. We go in search of items like food and even water. Can you believe that we have to scavenge in order to provide ourselves just with basic essentials like water? The most powerful military in the world, and we can't even get cigarettes and toilet paper.

Really, though, no one misses the stuff we grab. And besides, it's wrong how the food is not being distributed while we're starving. It's not as if we take from everyone. We never filch from other enlisted Marines, or grunts, as we like to call ourselves. We only scavenge from the guys who are hunkered down in the center of the base, or from the intelligence personnel or the air traffic controllers who are probably arranging for their buddies on the planes to fly in whatever they need.

It's not just food and supplies we take, either. A good example of how we've been left to fend for ourselves occurred when we began improving our lines right at the beginning of the siege. When we went to build our bunkers and dig out trenches, most of the tools and materials we used had to be "borrowed." The hierarchy had teams of engineers and Seabees building massive bunkers for the important guys, but there were just not enough engineers to go around. The military just did not have the resources for us to get any help or special tools. After all, for the most part we're just low-ranking kids, privates and corporals, who are here because we weren't able to afford college.

In the early stages of our tour, we were handed empty sandbags and in effect told, hey, you guys go do what you've got to do. Later, when we had to dig out our trenches so the incoming wouldn't kill us, the only things available to us with which to dig were E-tools, which are basically small shovels, our helmets, or our bare hands. We were not given picks, axes, or any other kinds of tools. We didn't have crap. We knew if we wanted to survive, we'd have to improvise or use any other techniques at our disposal to obtain what we needed, so I don't make any apologies for doing what's necessary for me to make it out of here alive.

Another item a lot of guys have acquired out of necessity is a Colt .45. Handguns are only issued to Marine officers, but because they're easier to use than an M-16 in close quarters, like in the trenches, everyone wants one. Since none of the grunts were issued handguns, some people have taken to stealing them.

Part of the problem is that many of us have developed the attitude that we are used like pawns in a giant chess match, and are being thrown just enough scraps so we won't completely starve. We feel that we're being treated as if we are expendable.

A big reason why we have developed this attitude, besides the way we are usually treated, lies in the layout of the base itself. The base is surrounded by rows of wire that stop right before our lines begin. Further inside the perimeter, past the trenches, is the area where all the officers live. In between the officers and us, though, is another line of coiled barbed wire and tanglefoot. In a way, we're trapped. If we're attacked, we sure as hell can't go forward, and we really can't move backwards, either. If we did, we would run right into the second line of wire.

Other aspects about the situation here really bother me, too. Being low men on the totem pole, we never really know exactly why we're carrying out our assignments. For example, if the sergeant comes to us and tells us to do something, we're expected to just obediently do it without question, even if that means we will be risking our lives for no apparent reason. We are never told why, or for what purpose, we should go out into the bush and risk being killed. There is hardly ever an explanation given for any of this madness. And considering that I'm putting my life on the line every second I'm here, maybe I would feel a little better about performing my duty, or at least not be so resentful, if I understood the object of all this.

Oh, there's one other thing that really pisses me off. I hate how officers are always coming around after the fact to pat guys on their back. They are never around when things are going down. Rarely do you ever see anyone higher than a lieutenant on the front lines. Even though they are invariably in the limelight, the generals and colonels are not the ones actually fighting the war, but they seem to take all the credit. Instead, the war is being fought by the grunts. It's young kids, hardly more than teenagers, really, who are putting their lives on the line. I'm sure there are older guys dying in Vietnam, too, and I am not trying to diminish the sacrifice they make, but all I see being spilled is the blood of the American kids, no older than eighteen or nineteen years old.

Well, enough complaining for now. Thanks for listening. It helps relieve some of the stress to get these things off my chest. I'll try and make sure that my next letter contains better news. Say hello to everyone for me, and I will write to you again soon.

Love,
Daniel

February 7, 1968

Dan turned up the volume on the command post radio, not believing what he was hearing. He looked at Robbie, whose complexion had turned pale, and then shifted his attention back to the radio. Even though moments of thick static interrupted the screaming and cries of terror, the events unfolding were all too clear. Looking around at the rest of the platoon, all of whom were now huddled near the radio, it was easy to see they all shared Dan's sense of horror. Second Platoon listened in despair to the most horrifying broadcast any of them had ever heard. Unfortunately, this was not an Orson Welles original.

"What the fuck, man?" Frazier blurted. "Why don't they fucking do something? We should be there helping. They're getting slaughtered."

As the broadcast continued, the platoon cringed as sounds of gunfire, grenade blasts, and the distant rumble of tanks mingled with the tone of terror and fear in the voices on the other end of the transmission. As he listened helplessly, Dan's blood boiled, and his mind filled with anger.

Just four miles to the west, the United States Special Forces camp at Lang Vei was under attack. The North Vietnamese Army was pushing through the base with a large contingent of foot soldiers, supported by a convoy of tanks. This marked the first instance the NVA was using tanks in the war, and they were proving deadly effective.

As Dan and his unit sat nervously, engrossed in the radio, the twenty-four Green Berets and 400 South Vietnamese and Montagnard irregulars at Lang Vei appealed for assistance, begging to be saved from almost certain death.

"Yo, Hanks," Dan screamed across the bunker, "Let's go help these guys. If we're not there soon, they'll all be dead."

"Calm down, Sullivan," Hanks yelled back. "All of you calm down. I just got off the line with the captain. He says no go. We stay put. There's nothing we can do."

"Fuck," yelled Evans. "Those are Americans there, and we're letting them get slaughtered."

"Damn it, Evans. Don't you see that's exactly what they want?" Hanks tried to explain. "Charlie is waiting for us to get on Route 9 and come to the rescue. They're waiting out there to ambush our asses. Then what? We'll all be dead!"

"This is bullshit," Evans blurted out, turning away in disgust.

All night the defenders of Lang Vei pleaded for help from Khe Sanh. But all night the Marines refused to send reinforcements. As a result, a majority of the soldiers at Lang Vei were killed. The Marines at Khe Sanh could do nothing but sit, helpless and terrified, listening as the Special Forces camp was razed to the ground.

In hindsight, the decision not to send reinforcements, though difficult to make, was correct. The NVA had, in fact, set up numerous ambushes along the route between Lang Vei and Khe Sanh, and was poised to blow away any Marine reinforcements.

The incident at Lang Vei served as a vivid reminder to the Marines at Khe Sanh of their own situation. Just as that night they were constrained from taking action while fellow Americans were being butchered only miles away, so too were they being forced to remain in their trenches at Khe Sanh without being allowed to defend themselves against the NVA incoming.

—

The casualties among the troops at Lang Vei were extensive. Of the twenty-four American Green Berets and 400 South Vietnamese and Montagnard irregulars defending the base that night, 255 were killed and another 77 were wounded.[2]

February 8, 1968

Robbie sat in the foxhole, leaning back against the dirt wall, his M-16 upright between his legs. His head was tilted upwards so that he could look at the night sky and stare at the stars. Fixated in this manner for several minutes, his gaze on the universe was eventually distracted by the clomping of approaching footsteps as Dan came over and sat down next to him.

"Hey, Danny, what do you think about?"

"What?" Dan replied, somewhat puzzled by the vagueness of the question. "What do you mean, 'What do I think about?'"

"Like when you're bored and just sittin' around."

"I don't know. Home, I guess. I think a lot about my family and friends. Sometimes, my mind wanders to girls, and frequently I find myself weighing my chances of making it out of here alive. I'm not sure. Why? What do you think about?"

"A lot of the same, I guess. It's that I was looking up at the sky and the stars, and it makes you realize how big this world is and how small we are." Robbie paused for a moment. "You know, I thought I could become a hero by joining the Marines and coming over here, but now I feel like I'm wasting my time. As you said to me weeks ago, there are no heroes here—only survivors. I don't know, maybe I'm just tired of this place."

Dan looked up to see a sky full of stars dotting the black heaven. He pulled out a cigarette and lit it, letting his mind fill with the sweet buzz of the tobacco. A couple of minutes later, it was his turn to break the silence.

"I got a letter from your sister yesterday. She talked a lot about your family's ranch and riding her horse. She said that when I get home, I have to come down to Texas and learn how to ride. As I read the letter, I could just picture her on a horse galloping across a wide-open and endless field of grass. The whole image was so clear in my mind. I just kept imagining how peaceful and beautiful it must be, to be where there is no war or violence."

"Silsbee really is a peaceful place, Dan. And more serene and beautiful than even the sky here."

"You want to know what I think about, Robbie? I think about how I can't wait to get home. That's all I want. I want to make it home alive. And once I've seen my family and told them how much I love them, I'll travel down to Silsbee and ride those horses."

February 10, 1968
Journal Entry

I was sitting in a foxhole this morning when Robbie approached with a huge metal can under his arm, and a big smile on his face. He told me about how the company gunny had come down and handed him a gigantic, cafeteria-style can of peaches, with orders that he was to offer it as a gift from the gunny to our lieutenant.

When I asked him why he had not yet given it to the lieutenant, he looked at me as if I'd lost my mind. As Robbie rightly pointed out, we hadn't eaten anything but C-rations since the siege began, and even with the C-rats, we are still always hungry. The gunny had to be crazy if he expected us to give away an entire can of peaches while we weren't getting shit to eat.

So, instead of giving the peaches to the lieutenant as ordered, Robbie and I ate them. The can must have been about a foot tall, and there were probably close to sixty sweet, syrupy peaches inside, but we managed to eat every last one. Robbie and I were as sick as dogs, and I never want to see, let alone eat, another peach in my life. Of course, later in the day the gunny stopped by to find out if the lieutenant liked his present. When the lieutenant learned from the gunny that we stole his gift, he chewed us out and threatened to make us spend the rest of our tour filling sandbags. Robbie and I didn't give a shit, though, because at least we weren't hungry anymore.

February 11, 1968
Dear Mom,
Besides dodging incoming and filling sandbags, there isn't much to do for excitement at Khe Sanh. For the most part, I'm either totally scared or completely bored out of my mind. Free time, of which there is plenty, is used to write letters, play cards, or just screw around. To help pass the hours, Robbie and I play tricks on our buddies or mess with the lifers. One of our favorite things to do is to go into the staff sergeant's bunker at night, while he's sleeping, and hide his equipment. A lot of my free time is spent reflecting about home and you guys. I also think a great deal about the war, and about this mess I'm in and how I'm going to make it out of here without getting killed. More than anything else, my main concern right now is making it home alive.

Another way we help to pass the time is by listening to the radio, especially to Hanoi Hannah. Every day, Hanoi Hannah, the voice of a North Vietnamese propaganda radio show, takes to the air and describes how the NVA is going to defeat the United States. She likes to go on about how we're all destined to die at the hands of her army, and that all the American soldiers are going home in body bags. We get a good laugh listening to her talk.

The show is mostly filled with this type of propaganda, so to get the Americans to listen, she plays popular music like Bob Dylan, the Rolling Stones, and the Beatles. What is great about the music is that much of what she spins is banned on the American armed forces radio station, Stars and Stripes, because of antiwar lyrics. As a result, the most popular radio program among our troops in Vietnam is not American, but a North Vietnamese propaganda show.

I actually have a funny story to tell you about Hanoi Hannah, related to the incoming. Since radio reception isn't very good at Khe Sanh, I decided to make a radio antenna, which I fashioned out of a wooden cross, wrapped with wire, so that our unit could pick up her broadcasts more clearly. One afternoon, while the fog was particularly bad, I climbed up onto the top of our bunker and stuck the makeshift antenna there. The static immediately vanished. As luck would have it, though, we were listening to a broadcast of Hanoi Hannah free of interference in reception for no more than fifteen minutes when incoming rounds started crashing into our area. The NVA thought the antenna meant our bunker was a communications outpost, and they were trying to cut off our contact with the outside world. Within a half-hour of setting up the antenna, I had pulled it down, and we resumed listening to Hanoi Hannah through static.

Since there is very little that one can do around here for entertainment without the risk of being killed, besides listening to the radio, guys have found creative ways to keep themselves amused. Some Marines wave "maggie drawers" from the trenches. Maggie drawers is the nickname for the flags waved on firing ranges when someone completely misses a target. At Khe Sanh, Marines with nothing better to do let NVA mortar gunners know when they missed their target by waving makeshift maggie drawers. There is one Marine in particular, serving in a unit located a couple of hundred yards down the trench line from our position, who has made this his favorite game. What he's done is tie a large rag onto a tent pole, and every time mortars land in his unit's area, you can see the flag protruding from the trenches, being waved back and forth. To let him know they are playing along, the NVA always pop off another round into the guy's area to thank him for letting them know they missed. . . .

Love,
Daniel

February 12, 1968
Journal Entry

I find that I'm not alone anymore in the constant struggle to keep up spirits. Everyone is trying desperately to find something—anything—to help maintain a positive outlook. Conditions are so poor, it's reached the point where even the tiniest bit of hope or seemingly good news can improve our morale. Something as simple as a pound cake or a couple of cigarettes in a box of C-rations can be enough to make it easier for us to get through a day. Letters from home, when they are actually delivered, always give a huge boost, and making off like a bandit with a lifer's C-rats or supplies serves to lift spirits, too.

A good rule of thumb as to the mood of the unit is that if we can go a couple of days without anyone being killed or badly hurt, then morale is high. On the other hand, if someone is blown away or wounded, morale tends to drop. Unfortunately, it seems like there are more days than not when we are dealing with a KIA or serious injuries.

Even I haven't escaped injury, although it was relatively minor. The other morning, the fog was extra thick, and so I foolishly thought it would be safe to take a quick walk around. I had been in the trenches for a couple of days straight, and desperately needed a change of scenery. I was out in the open for only a few minutes, going nowhere special, and the whole time paying extra close attention to my surroundings, keeping an eye on the fog, and listening for incoming. I had just decided it was time to get back below when I heard a mortar fired. I started to run for the trench line, but the round landed sooner than I expected and exploded nearby before I could make it into the trench. The shrapnel missed me, but the concussion still sent me flying hard into the side of our bunker. I went numb for a second upon impact, and then needles of pain shot through my entire body. I ended up with several severe bruises and a pretty badly gashed forehead.

Someone told me to put in for a Purple Heart, since after receiving three, you get to go home, but I'm not going to do that. I don't see how that would be fair. I don't believe I deserve the same medal as guys who are being shot up or blown apart, just for being thrown up against a bunker. Besides, I would have to be pretty lucky to make it to three Purple Hearts without getting killed. Whether it's shrapnel from incoming, getting shot by a sniper's bullet, or being blown to pieces by an artillery round, we are always right around the corner from meeting a fate worse by far than my close encounter. I know so because of the occasions when I have had to carry the limp, cold, lifeless body of a fallen friend to Graves Registration.

It's amazing how conditioned I have become to death. The reality is I don't even feel much sadness anymore from the sight of it. When I'm at Graves, sometimes I will linger, staring in silence at the green rubber body bags lying on the ground waiting to be picked up by the next available chopper. I still get upset and angry when I see a dead Marine, but at the same time, a part of me thinks, "Better him than me." Of course, I know this is the wrong way to feel, but maybe it's a survival instinct. I figure that if I'm surviving, I'm better off than if I were dead. I'm certainly not the only one who feels this way, either. No one wants their friends to die, but anyone telling the truth will admit they would always rather it be the other guy. I'm sure all this must sound screwed up, but I guess you wouldn't understand until you're in the situation yourself.

Regardless of these confused emotions, the morbid scenes of death that I witness almost every day are, without a doubt, the worst part of Nam. The lack of food and water, the terrible living conditions, the nasty weather, and the nearly overwhelming feelings of fear are all concerns I would rather contend with than the sight of a dead Marine. Sitting over a fallen comrade, holding his limp hands while waiting to put him on a stretcher, is the most sickening feeling in the world.

February 13, 1968
Dear Mom,

How are you doing? I know I have said it before, but I really do miss you guys a lot. I try to keep my mind off that subject, though, because being homesick is not a good frame of mind to be in here. So, guess what? I recently got some incredible news. Tomorrow, I'm getting the heck out of Khe Sanh, if only for a couple of days. I'm going on R&R for five days. That's five days of nothing to do but relax and not worry about being killed. I realize that it's going to be risky getting a flight off the base, but at this point, I'm willing to take the chance. It's very frustrating to be here. If only we could fight back, maybe it wouldn't be so bad. But we can't. Instead, all we can do is lay low and hope for the best. There isn't anyone to shoot at or fight with, and no way on our part to prevent our being fired upon. This whole experience is really just a big lesson in fear and frustration.

Well, enough of the doom and gloom. I just wanted to say hello and share the good news with you. I'll write again as soon as I return from R&R.

Love,
Daniel

February 20, 1968
Dear Mike,

Man, have I got some stories to tell you. I just got back from R&R, and it might have been the best five days of my life. It all started on the morning of the 14th, when I went down to the registry and cashed my service paychecks, which totaled close to $1,200. Then I went to the LZ to wait in the trenches off to the side of the runway for a ride. I knew it would be dangerous to try and leave, but I had to get the hell out of here. There were a couple of other Marines from other units there, too, and we passed the time shooting the shit and smoking cigarettes.

Eventually, after waiting into the afternoon, a chopper finally landed. Well, to be precise, it didn't really land as much as it touched down and just kept rolling along the runway. As I'm sitting there, waiting for it to stop, a couple of guys popped out of the trenches and started sprinting for the chopper. I sat there, hesitating for a moment, watching the helicopter roll past me. I was scared that if I got up to go for the chopper, a round would come in and kill me, but I also was aware that I wouldn't have many more chances to get off the base. After another moment of hesitation, I finally decided to go for it. Reasoning that I was going to get out of Khe Sanh or die trying, I leaped out of the trench, put my head down, and made a mad dash for the chopper. As I ran, I was terrified, and so intent on making it to the chopper that I never did take any time to consider the stupidity of what I was doing.

When I was twenty feet or so from the chopper, a round landed on the runway somewhere behind me. The explosion upon impact startled me so badly that, for all I know, I jumped those last twenty feet right into the helicopter. I got on board just in time, too, because about five seconds later, we were in the air. After a series of helicopter rides, I eventually made it to Da Nang, and from there I caught a flight into Hong Kong.

Mike, I'm telling you, Hong Kong might just be the greatest city in the world. There was food, beer, and women everywhere I went. The day I arrived, I checked into a hotel and took my first shower in over a month. It felt so good to stand under the water and get myself clean, although afterwards I still felt dirty, even after having scrubbed myself twice. After I dried off and put on a fresh change of clothes that I had picked up in Da Nang, I went down to the hotel bar and had the most delicious meal. Oh, man, had I missed real food. After dinner, I sat at the bar drinking with a couple of guys stationed in Vietnam who were also on R&R. While we drank, two somewhat elderly Chinese men approached and sat down right next to us, even though there was plenty of room at the other end of the bar.

It was not lost on the three of us that being young American males, sporting crew cuts and tattoos, it was easy for strangers to recognize that we served in the military. This made me nervous, because at Khe Sanh there are rumors circulating that the Chinese are helping the North Vietnamese war effort. I became paranoid about these two men being near us, and when I tried to get them to go away, one of them reached into a leather satchel he was carrying. Instinctively, the three of us leaped off our stools and tackled the guy, thinking he was reaching for a gun or a bomb. One of the waiters quickly came running over, and in broken English kept repeating the words "Hong Kong custom suit" and showed us that all the old man was trying to do was pull out his tape measure. We now understood that these two Chinese men were just simple tailors who made their living roaming around from bar to bar selling suits to American military personnel. Anyway, since I felt badly about almost killing the one tailor, and inasmuch as I had a ton of cash on me, I decided to buy a suit.

The guy took my measurements, left the bar, and a couple of hours later came back with this gorgeous, handmade suit. For around fifty American dollars, I got the suit, a dress shirt, a tie, and shoes. The suit even fit me well, too. Unfortunately, it didn't make it through the week. I wore it so often and spilled so much shit on it that by the time I left Hong Kong, I ended up throwing it away. I got my money's worth out of it, though, and besides, what was I going to do with a suit at Khe Sanh?

After dinner and having the suit delivered to me, I spent the rest of that first night in Hong Kong going from bar to bar with some other Marines I had met after leaving the hotel, getting lit, and picking up women. Each night thereafter was almost a carbon copy, with food, drinking, and lots of partying. It seemed like anything we wanted or desired was ours to have. I had left Khe Sanh with close to $1,200, and by the end of R&R, I spent nearly all of it. I'm not joking, bro. I blew almost every single dollar, but it was totally worth it. I've never had a better time in my life.

After the five days I spent in Hong Kong, it really sucks being back here at Khe Sanh. But this is where I need to be right now. I have heard that some guys who take R&R make their way to Hong Kong and then just disappear into opium dens, or bribe their way onto a cargo ship headed for some far away country, but I could never do something like that. I'm sure you think I'm probably crazy for coming back, but my unit is here, and I would never abandon them. I just couldn't do that to my friends. I will talk to you later, Mike. And remember, no matter what you do, don't enlist, because you don't want to be here.

    Take care,
    Danny

February 21, 1968

The Khe Sanh Combat Base was now under siege for a month.

February 23, 1968

On February 23, the Khe Sanh Combat Base received 1,307 rounds of incoming.[3] The majority of these rounds landed during the afternoon hours, after the cloud cover had lifted. During this portion of the day, the base received an average of five to six rounds per minute.[4] It was the heaviest barrage of any one single day during the siege, and resulted in the death of ten Marines, with another fifty-one seriously injured.[5]

Dan returned from R&R to find conditions and morale at the base had deteriorated dramatically in just the few days that he was away. The situation at Khe Sanh had reached a new low point.

♠

Chapter 8

-Late February/Early March-

"You always write it's bombing, bombing, bombing. It's not bombing, it's air support."
    -U.S. Air Force Colonel David Opfer, air attaché in Cambodia, complaining to reporters about their coverage of the Vietnam War.

February 26, 1968
Journal Entry

As part of the guerrilla warfare training we received during advanced training at Camp Pendleton last October, Robbie and I were put through a prisoner of war course. Included in the course was a field exercise where we were taken prisoner by Marine instructors posing as enemy soldiers, and physically abused by our captors by being deprived of sleep, food, and water. After about a day of this role-playing, we were allowed to escape, and then we were expected to make our way through the woods to a checkpoint several miles away. We had received advance warning that we could run into ambushes while heading back to the checkpoint, and we were cautioned to keep an eye out and make every effort to avoid them. The Marines staging the ambushes were only going to be firing blanks, but if fired upon we would be considered casualties and have to surrender.

To make the exercise as realistic as possible, we were forbidden from bringing any food or water. However, Robbie and I decided we weren't interested in playing along with that particular restriction, and so the night before the exercise we went to the PX and bought a bunch of "pogie bait," candy bars and other junk food, that we stuffed into the pockets of our pants.

When the two of us left the mock POW camp together the next day, we headed out into the woods. We were ditty-bopping toward the checkpoint, eating our pogie bait, enjoying the scenery, and generally goofing off, when suddenly an ambush opened up on us with their M-

16s. Blanks or no blanks, Robbie and I were scared half to death by the unanticipated burst of gunfire. Instinctively, we acted to defend ourselves, but with no weapons of our own, we had to improvise. The two of us picked up golf ball and baseball-sized rocks from the forest floor, and started throwing them in the direction of the ambush. We eventually surrendered, but not before we had scored some direct hits and angered a few of the Marines.

Looking back on that training exercise, never in my wildest imagination did I ever expect to be in a situation, like the one that I experienced yesterday, where I might actually have to apply the lessons taught during that course at Camp Pendleton.

February 25, 1968
<u>1/26 Marines Command Chronology</u>

At 0730H, a platoon sized patrol departed on a security patrol to the southeast of the Khe Sanh Combat Base.

—

On the morning of February 25, 3rd Platoon, Bravo Company, led by Lieutenant Don Jacques, departed the base on patrol. Jacques had received orders to escort his platoon to find an enemy mortar gun that had been firing into the perimeter of the base. First and Second Platoons, Bravo Company, were ordered to serve as standby reinforcements for 3rd Platoon in case the latter should get into trouble. Jacques led 3rd Platoon to the southeast end of the runway, and from there guided them in a southwesterly direction beyond the perimeter. Once they left the base, 1st Platoon took over the position at the end of the runway and eventually headed off the base in a southerly direction.

While conducting the sweep, the Jacques patrol spotted three North Vietnamese soldiers walking in a clearing. Observing the three NVA troops, Jacques ordered his troops to capture them, hoping the enemy combatants might be able to provide valuable intelligence. On Jacques' command, the Marines of 3rd Platoon began to give chase, unaware that they never stood a chance of capturing the three decoys. Moments after initiating their pursuit, the entire platoon ran directly into an NVA ambush, and within minutes, twenty-five Marines were dead.

1/26 Marines Command Chronology

Bravo Company, 3rd Platoon spotted three NVA in the open, moved toward them and were hit by NVA in a trench. NVA automatic weapons and 50 caliber fire and 30 caliber fire pinned down the front and left flank. Tried to pull back and were hit by sniper fire.

1/26 Marines Command Chronology - 1530H

[1st platoon Company B.] moved out of gate 42 with 1st and 2nd squads: action force (B1) and B3 engaged themselves in a firefight to their direct front. Received small arms fire from approximately 20 meters from dug in automatic weapons. These positions were approximately 600 meters from bunker 42. We held up and returned fire. Took incoming rockets and mortars in 2nd squad position. We withdrew from area to the trench line, while still under fire. First and second squads returned fire on enemy, dug into trench lines. On orders withdrew with as many WIAs as we could locate.

February 26, 1968
Journal Entry (continued)

. . . We heard massive amounts of gunfire coming from in front of us, and then large-scale confusion was transmitted over the radio. Third Platoon was coming under intense fire from an NVA U-shaped ambush. Our lieutenant started screaming at us to move out and help them, and so we went charging into the jungle, which was exactly what the NVA wanted. They were just lying in wait for us, and as soon as we were within range, they let us have it.

We received heavy fire from NVA soldiers hiding in trenches that were somehow dug in the vicinity of the base without us ever knowing of the enemy activity. Everyone around me was scattering, ducking for cover, or simply dropping to the ground to avoid getting shot. It all happened so quickly, though, that some Marines were hit before they could even react.

We were completely disorganized, and it immediately became obvious that it was now every man for himself. Total disorder reigned. Everything that we had ever learned in training about how to react when under attack went out of the window. We were just trying to get our asses out of the line of fire. I was panicked. It was all I could do to keep firing my weapon and changing clips. Anything that moved, I shot at. The situation was really ugly. A guy next to me took some grenade shrapnel in his hand. He dropped his weapon, picked it up in the other hand, and began firing again. His wounded hand was a bloody pulp, but he knew that if he stopped shooting, he'd be dead.

Eventually, someone started yelling for us to withdraw to the base. Guys turned tail and began a cautious retreat, which is pretty much what I did, too. There were NVA everywhere, darting through the jungle shooting at us. Some NVA were close enough that I could actually see their faces. Somehow, I managed to join up with Robbie, J.R., and Emmett. We tried to make our way back to the base, but it didn't take long before we realized that we were surrounded. The NVA were all over the fucking place. They had overrun our lines. We were trapped. If we tried to get back into the base, they would see us, and we would be easy targets. I was really afraid I was going to die. We all were.

Not wanting to remain exposed to the NVA, we scrambled into an area with lots of cover and hid out. We didn't have a radio, so we couldn't communicate our location to anyone on base. Even if the base knew exactly where we were, we would probably still have been on our own. I could hear Charlie talking all around us, and recognized that we would be committing suicide if we tried to move further. There was no other choice but to stay quiet and not do a goddamn thing. The four of us laid on our stomachs and, in low whispers, tried to come to some agreement about what our next action should be. We felt so scared and powerless. Even though we considered that the NVA might be walking around killing our guys who were wounded and needed medical attention to survive, we were helpless to do anything to assist. We couldn't take the risk of giving ourselves away, or we would have surely been killed, too. All of us had heard the stories of how North Vietnamese soldiers would torture and then kill American soldiers they caught in the bush. We'd even heard rumors about how the NVA would cut off our balls and stick them in our mouths, so we kept really fucking quiet.

Our biggest challenge became figuring out how to get safely back inside our own wire. Aside from having to worry about the NVA, we also were uneasy about the possibility of being shot by our own people. If we came crawling through the wire and were not recognized as friendlies, we were likely to be hit by one of our own. The four of us laid there in the same position for hours, evaluating our options. Robbie and I kept making eye contact with one another, aiming to reassure the other by looking brave. Still, I could tell he was frightened. But then again, so was I. Even though we were all terrified, each of us did our best to project courage because we knew it was necessary to show strength if we wanted to make it back alive.

When it got dark, we decided we had to make our move, or by morning we would be dead. Moving very slowly, and very, very carefully, we managed to approach the perimeter. It took us two hours to crawl a couple of hundred yards. As we crawled, what concerned me most was that at any moment we might come across a group of NVA and have no alternative but to attempt to shoot our way back onto the base. We knew NVA soldiers were still in the area, because we had heard them talking all through the evening. As I continued crawling, I imagined them sitting in the bush, setting their traps for us to fall into, and the thought scared the hell out of me.

As we neared the wire, we realized we were not alone in trying to get back onto the base. It soon became obvious that many of the Marines who survived the firefight that morning were not able to reach the base during daylight. Not wanting to risk moving around in the jungle during the day, they had also hidden outside the wire. Because many of those on the patrol had not yet made it back, Marines on the base were put on shifts to wait for us. The four of us made it onto the base sometime after midnight, but some guys did not make it back until the next morning.

Reflecting on what happened, the whole maneuver was fucked-up. There was no organization whatsoever, and it basically ended up being a bunch of eighteen and nineteen-year-old privates left to fend for themselves. It was planned poorly, run badly, and guys ended up being killed for nothing.

1/26 Marines Command Chronology

```
    Contact   resulted   in   24   friendly   MIA,   17
friendly WIA, and six friendly KIA.
```

Except for the body of Lieutenant Don Jacques, the bodies of the twenty-five Marines killed in the initial ambush were not recovered until April.

February 28, 1968
Dear Mike,
. . . As the siege has progressed, the trenches we are living in have become unbelievably unsanitary and filthy, filled with waste and human excrement. As you might imagine, with all the trash, the trenches have become infested with giant rats in search of food. The rats are always scurrying through the lines and coming into our bunkers to mill around and scavenge. They are really bold, too, never seeming to mind our presence. It's almost as if we aren't even there. They just parade about in the open, acting like they own the place. I've even seen them walk across guys who are sleeping.

Because the rats are such a problem, many of us are using them as target practice for newly acquired .45s. So now we are exposed to yet another danger due to Marines indiscriminately shooting at rats scampering through the trenches. It is especially bad at night, when the rats really come out in force. We've actually had an instance or two of guys being shot at by members of their own units while walking around at night, because in the darkness the moving shadows were mistaken for giant rodents.

I recently got myself into trouble doing something similar. One night last week, I was standing at the end of our trench line going to the bathroom, holding my .45, which I have gotten into the habit of taking with me wherever I go. I was just finishing up, when all of a sudden I heard a noise behind me. It startled the crap out of me, and I turned around expecting to see a rat. Instead, I observed the silhouette of what appeared to be a North Vietnamese soldier. My first thought was that the NVA had penetrated our lines, and instinctively I raised my gun and fired several times. Because it was so dark, I ended up missing every shot, and the guy went scurrying for his life. After I settled down and realized we weren't being attacked, it dawned on me that I might have shot at an ARVN soldier who strayed from his own lines. The next day my suspicion was confirmed when a lieutenant chewed me out over the incident. Not that I, or anyone else, really cared, since the ARVN aren't very well liked around here anyway. . . .

Take care,
Danny

March 1, 1968
1/26 Marines Command Chronology

    `From the 37th ARVN Ranger Battalion: have unknown size NVA force making probe in front of our position.`

—

In a brazen assault on the night of March 1, the NVA attacked the ARVN lines and penetrated their section of the base perimeter. The ARVN, who were known among the Marines to retreat in the face of pressure, lived up to their reputation in this instance. In light of the fact that Charlie Company's lines tied in with those of the ARVN, Dan's unit was ordered to fill in areas that the ARVN had vacated.

During the ensuing melee, Dan found himself in a fighting hole along the ARVN lines, firing his weapon at an NVA unit in the wire. Suddenly, he heard someone running behind him through the trenches, and then the unmistakable sound of an AK-47 being fired. Dan turned around and clearly saw an NVA soldier running past. He sprang out of his hole and lowered his M-16, but as he did so, a Marine in the next foxhole cut down the intruder. The enemy soldier fell against the trench wall and tumbled to the ground. Breathing a slight sigh of relief, Dan looked at the lifeless body for a second, and then jumped back into his foxhole.

The fighting on this particular night was prolonged and intense, and there were several recorded incidents of hand-to-hand combat in the trenches, with Marines using bayonets and E-tools to defend themselves. By morning, the NVA had been repelled from the base, but once again, just as had occurred on February 25, bloodshed and confusion marked the battle.

March 2, 1968
Journal Entry

The NVA incoming continues to be relentless. There's one North Vietnamese mortar gunner in particular who sits in front of our position and has been bugging us for weeks. Each morning, without fail, whoever is working the gun pops off a couple of mortars. Then, right about noon, he shoots off a couple of more rounds, and for good measure, around dinner, he fires off one or two more. It's gotten to where I can tell the time of day by these mortar attacks.

Every day we launch artillery, call in air strikes, and fire off quad 50 and mortar rounds on the gunner's position, but no matter what we do, we can't seem to kill the son of a bitch. To add insult to injury, not long after every one of our air strikes or artillery barrages, he pops off a few more rounds just to let us know he's still alive and kicking.

March 3, 1968

"Full house. I win," Robbie said, reaching for the pot to collect his winnings, which consisted of several cigarettes and a couple of packs of gum.

"Robbie, you must be cheating or something, man. That's the third hand in a row you've won," Rodriguez complained. "I give up. You guys are taking all my smokes."

"Well, I'm still in," J.R. declared, collecting the cards. "I have to win my stuff back. Who's still playing? Dan?"

"Yeah, I'm still in," Dan replied.

"Hey, deal me in, too," Roland told J.R. as he entered the bunker. J.R. shuffled the cards and dealt a new hand.

"Hey, can you guys believe Harris?" Professor asked, shifting the topic of conversation as he put down the book he was reading. "I never thought he was going to leave this place."

"No kidding," Robbie agreed. "It took five of us to persuade him to get on the chopper. He didn't even take his gear with him. He thought it would slow him down while he was running across the LZ."

"Hey, that's what happens to a guy when he gets short," Dan added matter-of-factly. "Your mind starts playing with you. I mean, the guy was in Nam for more than a year, and he finally gets to go home. How much would it suck to die the day you were leaving? I know that's exactly how he was thinking, too. Give me three cards, J.R."

Outside, an explosion went off in the distance. Hardly anyone noticed.

"Hey, man. Harris nearly lost it," Rodriguez said as he counted his remaining cigarettes. "It's crazy how a guy will get short and only have a week or so left, and it changes his whole mentality. Robbie and I pleaded with him to go outside to piss, and he said he'd kill us if we tried to use physical force to make him. I believed him when he said it, too. He didn't even go on an LP for the last three weeks, and before yesterday, he hadn't left the bunker for two weeks."

Robbie asked for two cards and resumed the conversation. "I can't really blame him. Y'all know how it is. It's dangerous getting in and out of here. Even if you do get a plane to touch down, it won't stop. You have to keep running after it, and then you gotta jump to get on board."

"I fold," Roland said, dropping his cards.

"And don't forget," Robbie continued, "while all that's going on, you have to hope incoming doesn't kill you. I can understand Harris' fears. Shit, I'll probably be the same way when I get ready to leave. If Charlie doesn't get you while you're here, he'll try to nail you when you're leaving."

"All right," announced J.R., changing the topic back to the card game. "All bets in. Let's see what each of you has."

"I've got aces and eights," Robbie stated with a wide grin.

Everyone else took a quick look at their cards and then threw them down in disgust. Robbie just chuckled as he gathered up his winnings of cigarettes and gum.

—

One of the historically significant military accomplishments linked to the siege of Khe Sanh was the unprecedented use of air support by the American forces in the defense of the base. Never before had the world witnessed such military power and intensity from the air. Air Force F-100s, and Navy and Marine F-4 fighter-bombers and A-4 light bombers, would fly under the overcast skies above Khe Sanh dropping napalm and finned bombs over enemy entrenchments and hideaways.[1] Pinpoint accuracy allowed these aircraft to drop their bombs as close as 100 yards to the base perimeter. Dozens of these tactical air raids were flown each day, destroying enemy trenches that were constantly forming around the base.

It was the B-52 bombing raids, however, that provided the most impressive display of American aerial force. "Arc lights," the military's term for B-52 bombing raids, were instrumental in the defense of Khe Sanh. By reason of the fact that they flew at an altitude of 40,000 feet, arc lights could completely avoid the reach of enemy guns, as well as cause an otherwise dangerous cloud ceiling to become inconsequential. Given that the B-52s were able to make their bombing runs regardless of any difficulties presented by the weather and enemy fire, as many as forty to fifty arc lights could occur over Khe Sanh during any single day.

The destructive power of an arc light was unmatched by other conventional weapons. Flying all the way from airbases on the Pacific island of Guam, the B-52s would drop their arsenal of 500 and 750-pound bombs on unsuspecting North Vietnamese soldiers, leaving total destruction in their wake.[2] The bombs would produce craters the size of houses, and when the B-52s completed a mission, whole areas of jungle would be left destroyed. The B-52s systematically pattern bombed suspected enemy positions, using a radar process called "sky spotting" that directed the planes over the general target area.[3] This system allowed for such accuracy by American pilots that the arc light could be carried out within several hundred yards of the Khe Sanh Combat Base. Arc lights truly mixed an impressive combination of destructive firepower and pinpoint accuracy.

The results of the B-52 bombing raids were astounding. The enemy had to face not only the physical effects of the total devastation and death the arc lights produced, but also the equally destructive psychological effects. Inasmuch as the B-52s flew at such a high altitude, they could neither be seen nor heard from the ground. Consequently, the North Vietnamese soldiers who died from the arc lights never knew what hit them. Living with the fear of instantaneous death played heavily on the minds of the enemy, prompting many North Vietnamese to abandon their posts. One NVA soldier, who surrendered to American forces fearing he would become a victim of the B-52s, claimed that three-fourths of his unit of 2,000 had died as a result of arc lights.[4]

March 6, 1968

Dear Mom,

. . . It's truly indescribable what happens when they carry out one of these bombing raids. When they tell us an arc light is coming, everyone is supposed to put on their helmets and flak jackets and get down in the trenches. Of course, nobody listens to the second part of the instructions because everyone wants to see the arc lights, and so we always try to peek over the trenches to watch what happens. At the same time, we have to stay on our toes and be ready to duck for cover, since some of the raids are so close that debris will come flying into our lines.

Even though we know the B-52s are up there, we can't see them because they are flying too high, but as the bombs are about to land, we hear this weird noise, kind of like a creaky door opening. Then, all of a sudden, the earth lifts up, as if it's exploding from within. Bright flashes of light that engulf the entire horizon, followed by huge plumes of smoke that appear to reach up to the sky, occur after the explosions. When the raids are near enough, the ground under us will shake as I imagine it would during an earthquake. I mean, it is just unbelievable how much power and destructiveness these bombs generate.

I believe that if not for the Air Force and all the bombs they drop, we would undoubtedly be getting our butts kicked. Every day, there are repeated air strikes on the NVA forces surrounding the base, and this is probably the only tactic keeping them at bay. It seems like Charlie knows that if he advances too far forward, our Air Force will get him.

I've got to tell you, I have a lot of respect for the pilots who fly those planes, because what they do is really hazardous. I have already seen two Phantoms and an F-4 go down in our area. I actually watched one of the Phantoms get hit. I could see the NVA tracer bullets go right through the back of the plane, and then smoke started coming out of the engine. The pilot circled the base once, pointed the plane into the jungle, and ejected over the base. He was so close, we waved to him as he parachuted safely onto the base. . . .

Love,
Daniel

March 17, 1968

Dear Mom,

Well, I recently learned the hard way just how much respect the rats at Khe Sanh have for the Marines. I have told you before about how huge and nasty they are—I mean, they'll open your C-rations for you. Anyway, a week ago, I was in the bunker when a rat appeared out of nowhere and, in broad daylight, bit a Marine named Artie on the arm. I guess the NVA figure if they can't finish us off with their bullets and bombs, then they'll send their pets after us. Artie had to be medevaced off the base for shots because our corpsmen are afraid the rats around here have rabies. He ended up being flown all the way to a hospital in Da Nang due to the rabies serum requiring refrigeration, and there hasn't been electricity at Khe Sanh since January.

Of course, getting him off the base was no easy task. It is still quite dangerous trying to fly in and out of Khe Sanh. The medevac chopper on which he departed the base had flown in to pick up some of the more seriously wounded Marines, and was an inviting target for the NVA. While it was being loaded with the injured, several rounds landed on the runway, but luckily they didn't hit anything but dirt.

When Artie returned to Khe Sanh a few days later, he admitted that while aboard the chopper, he had felt very awkward sitting there next to guys with shrapnel or bullet wounds. He said you could tell that some of them were in a serious world of hurt. . . .

Love,
Daniel

♠

Chapter 9

-Robbie-

"If I had to choose between betraying my country and betraying my friend, I hope I should have the guts to betray my country."

— E.M. Forster

March 22, 1968
Journal Entry

At dusk, I set off on an LP with Robbie and two others. Sometime before midnight, after hours of an uneasy silence, we heard movement in front of our position. Everyone was on edge because there were rumors circulating that the NVA might attack the base to coincide with the anniversary of the March 1954 assault at Dien Bien Phu. As a precautionary measure, command ordered us to return to base so that if an assault did occur, we wouldn't be caught alone outside the wire. We made it back inside the perimeter and to our lines without any difficulty, but then Robbie and I did something very unusual for the two of us—we split up. I went into the trenches and Robbie headed to our platoon bunker. As we parted, he said only that he would rejoin me in a minute.

Everything remained quiet on the base for a short time as I situated myself in a foxhole. A few minutes passed, and Robbie had not yet returned, when suddenly the North Vietnamese started pummeling us with a heavy barrage of incoming. Within seconds, I heard an artillery round hit to my right, over toward our bunker. It impacted with a deafening sound, shaking the ground fiercely. My gut told me that the round had landed way too close for comfort, and I immediately scrambled to the top of the trench so that I could see what damage was done. What I saw when I looked in the direction of the bunker made my heart sink. Even in the darkness I could make out that the whole structure was smoking, and noticed small flames dancing from the wreckage. A large chunk of runway matting was sticking up from where the roof had once rested, and twisted metal and debris was scattered everywhere.

Our guys had worked hard to build that bunker so it would provide as much protection as possible, but despite all our earlier efforts, the bunker was completely destroyed. Even with all the runway matting we managed to scavenge, and all the sandbags we had filled, we could never have used enough material to turn aside the direct hit the bunker had just taken from the NVA artillery round.

My first thought was of Robbie. I feared that he lay buried somewhere underneath all that destruction, and so I jumped out of the trench and ran to the bunker as fast as my legs could move. The incoming was intensifying, with explosions resonating every few seconds or so, but I no longer cared about my own safety. I grabbed the very first piece of metal I could reach, and simultaneously started pulling and praying. The rest of the unit joined me, and we all began to frantically dig out the bunker with our bare hands, oblivious to the risk of injuring ourselves on the splintered wood and razor sharp edges of metal.

After a few minutes of digging, one of the other guys found Robbie. I stopped what I was doing and moved quickly to help get him free. But it was too late. Robbie was dead.

When the artillery round hit, the bunker's roof was shredded like wet newspaper. The explosion tore through the interior, ripping down the support beams and causing the roof to collapse. The entire structure was totally demolished. The Marines inside probably had no time to react, the roof falling on top of them before they could realize their situation. Death had to have come quickly. I took little solace from knowing that Robbie, in all likelihood, never knew what hit him.

Once we managed to get him loose from underneath a bunch of tangled wood, I grabbed Robbie under the armpits and lifted his limp body out of the debris. Carefully, I laid him out on the ground next to where the bunker had stood. My initial thought was that I really didn't want Robbie to be dead. For a second, I hoped it might all be a dream, and that I would wake up and he and I could hang out again. A few seconds later, when that moment passed and reality hit me, I became really fucking pissed off. But the shock of seeing Robbie lying there, dead at my feet, was nearly too much for me to handle. First, my body felt weak, and I briefly became sick to my stomach. Then I was rocked by dizziness, as if I had been punched in the head, and I thought for an instant that my legs might give out from under me. As I struggled to cope with my physical reactions, I became all choked up. My mind filled with thoughts of sadness, helplessness, and despair. A dozen or so Marines were within twenty feet of where I stood, but fortunately, not one of them said a word to me. If any one of them had, I don't think I would have been able to respond intelligently.

Staring in disbelief at Robbie's body, my grief rapidly turned to anger. Looking deep into his still, emotionless eyes, all I could now contemplate was how the NVA were killing guys every single day, and we weren't being allowed to do a damn thing about it. My fists were clenched in rage, and somewhere in the back of my mind I had a vision of picking up my M-16 and heading off alone into the jungle to kill anything that I could find.

My eyes turned back to Robbie. I felt like crying.

—

REPORT OF CASUALTY

CO C 1ST BN 26TH MAR   3D MAR DIV

CASSIDY Robbie Jason

1436919/0321   PFC   USMC

Died 22Mar68 Quang Tri Province republic of Vietnam result fragmentation wounds to the head from hostile artillery fire while in a defensive position.

1/26 Marines Command Chronology
2350H- received an unknown amount of incoming artillery and rockets including a hit on Company C Command Post. Unknown amount of Fr/WIA's and KIA's at this time.

March 23, 1968
Journal Entry

This morning I got to see Robbie's body in the light. He was still lying on the ground where he was placed last night. The weather was damp and foggy, and I could hear gunfire somewhere in the distance, although I paid little attention to any of it. I just stared at Robbie and cried quietly to myself. I hadn't realized the extent of his injuries last night in the darkness, but I could see now that the top of his head was missing. Blood trickled down his face from his head wound, reminding me of drops of water running down a windowpane. After a few moments I moved closer to him, and for reasons I'm not sure I could possibly explain, I put my foot next to his head and let the blood drip onto my boot.

I took a moment to look away and compose myself, and when I turned back a minute later, it hit me that Robbie's body was not lying alone. It had been a nasty night, and the Charlie Company Command Post, which was right down the line from our position, had also taken a direct hit.

Placed near Robbie was the body of a captain I had never seen before, as well as that of a gunnery sergeant, who I had noticed on occasion around the base, but hardly knew. That I did not know either of them, or that they were not grunts, did not make me any less saddened by their deaths.

Lieutenant Spruce was lying there, too. Even though he was an officer, he was one of the few who had always seemed to show a genuine interest in the well-being of the grunts. For that I respected him, and was truly sorry to see him dead.

Finally, there was Lance Hayduke. Lance had completed his tour of duty just yesterday, and was supposed to have left for the States. He had spent a good part of the day waiting on the flight deck, attempting to get out of Khe Sanh, but was unable to catch a ride. Rather than remain in the trenches by the runway, he had decided to spend the night back in the lines, thinking it would be safer. He should have been on his way home by now.

I turned my attention back to Robbie. He was my best friend, and it tore me up inside to see him like this. I already missed him deeply, and I wanted him back. At the same time, I was angry. I felt the urge to retaliate against the people who had done this to him. I wanted some payback.

A minute or so later, I knelt down, covered Robbie with a poncho, and whispered a final goodbye to him.

March 24, 1968

Dear Mr. and Mrs. Cassidy,

My name is Daniel Sullivan, and I served with your son Robbie in Vietnam. I am writing to tell you how very sorry I am for your loss, and how much of an honor it was to have known Robbie.

With all the terrible events I have experienced during my tour in Vietnam, the strong friendships that I have developed with the Marines in my unit are often the only thing that helps me make it through each day. The guys that I live with are my closest friends, and the people I know and trust. They are my brothers and my blood. We take care of and protect one another, doing our utmost to watch each other's back, and to keep each other mentally strong in the face of adversity. We have been brought together into the fire of hell, and sometimes it seems that these relationships are the last remaining bit of good that has survived our time here.

The story of my best friendship in Vietnam actually started before I arrived in-country. It dates back to when I was assigned to infantry training in North Carolina. There, in the sweltering summer heat of the first day of training, I met your son. During our stay in North Carolina, we would hang out together every evening, either going to the movies or just talking about life over a beer. I admired that Robbie was a down-to-earth, all around nice guy, and during the two weeks we spent in North Carolina, it seemed as if we were together constantly. We became the best of friends in just that short period of time.

Our friendship grew strong despite the numerous obvious differences between us. Your son was raised in Silsbee, Texas, and in many ways was the typical hillbilly boy who spoke with a heavy southern accent and loved listening to country music. I grew up in the city of

Philadelphia, using expressions like "yo," and developing a passion for classic rock n' roll. He liked riding horses, playing football, and reading books. I liked cars and baseball, and was content, to Robbie's dismay, with reading the box scores of baseball games. But all these differences never seemed to matter to either of us.

When infantry training ended, we were to meet up again at advanced training at Camp Pendleton, California. Eventually, the two of us were assigned not only to the same Marine division, but also the same regiment, battalion, company, platoon, and even squad. And despite the unbelievable odds of this occurring, considering all the different assignments we each could have received, Robbie and I ended up together in the trenches of Vietnam.

If at any time we were separated as a result of being assigned to different units, we would have gone our separate ways, and it is unlikely we would have been able to keep in close contact. However, as fate and luck would have it, we never parted, and our friendship continued to strengthen.

Being together at Khe Sanh, Robbie and I had numerous opportunities to talk with each other. Much of that time, we would discuss home and family. I remember how Robbie would always speak about you, Mr. Cassidy, and how proud he was that you were a war hero. He told me stories that described growing up in Silsbee, and always asked about Philadelphia and what it was like to live there. Robbie was very curious about my home life. Since Silsbee is sort of in the middle of nowhere, and because he had never spent any time in a big city, such concepts as row homes, street blocks, and neighborhoods, all very common to Philadelphia, amazed and intrigued him. For Robbie, Philadelphia was a world as far away from Silsbee as was Vietnam.

When not talking about home, and to keep from becoming bored while biding our time here, we would pull pranks and play practical jokes on officers. Besides hanging out together and getting into mischief, the two of us frequently worked side by side, whether we were filling sandbags or going into the bush on patrol. Whenever we went into the jungle together, we were intent on watching each other's back. After circumstances on the base really deteriorated, at night the two of us would go and hunt for things like food and supplies. We were resourceful and cunning, and together made a successful team. Please don't think of your son as a thief, though, Mrs. Cassidy. He wasn't. He was a survivor. After conditions turned desperate on base, scavenging became a way of life, a necessity in order to survive both physically and emotionally. It helped our morale that we were able to acquire basic items, like food and clothing, which helped make our lives here somewhat bearable. We were a couple of teenagers making the best of an awful situation.

One memento that Robbie carried around with him was a picture of his sister, your daughter, posing with your family horse. Robbie encouraged me to write her, and I have looked forward to receiving her letters during my tour of duty here. I would like to write her now, but I don't know what I would say to her. I am sure she must be very upset about all this. I hope you will pass on these words to her for me.

Maybe I really don't know what to say to the two of you, either. I want to express something that will make your loss less painful, but I suppose even a great writer might never come up with adequate words. I guess all I can say is that I am sorry. I mourn for your loss, and regret that there was not more I could have done to help Robbie. But it really doesn't accomplish anything to say that, because it won't bring him back.

Robbie and I laughed with each other in our times of joy, and we tried to be strong for one another in our times of fear. We were inseparable. I sit here and smile thinking of his memory, knowing that I will miss him very much.

Very truly yours,
Private 1st Class Daniel J. Sullivan

—

Dan stared at the letter as it went up in flames, the lighter still burning in his hand. Although he had spent hours trying to compose the words so they would be just right, ultimately he could not bring himself to mail out the letter. As he watched the flames dance from the last bit of paper, he dropped the remains of the letter to the ground, reached out with his foot, and extinguished the scraps with the heel of his boot. He then wiped the tears from his cheeks and lit a cigarette. Despite all that he had written, in the end, the words were empty. Nothing he could put down on paper would do his feelings justice. He knew that no matter how long he sat and wrote, he would never gather the right words to express to Robbie's family how truly sorry he was.

—

There were other friends besides Robbie, guys like Anthony "Doc" Vaccaro, a Navy corpsman from Wilmington, Delaware, and Billy Chamberlain, one of the few married men Dan met in the trenches, and who constantly talked about his wife. Dan fondly recalls Frank "Frankie" Rodriguez, born in Mexico and raised in California, who was serving his second tour of duty while at Khe Sanh. And there was Eli Hanks, who hailed from upstate Pennsylvania and at the age of twenty-one, with a couple of tours completed, was considered by the younger grunts to be an experienced Marine.

Dan's friends came with all sorts of personalities. Emmett Lawton was a likeable but nervous sort who loved country music, despite being raised not in the South, but in New York State, and Jimmy Doyle, a big, strapping kid, could always be overheard telling jokes. Although most of Dan's friends were grunts, Second Lieutenant Mark Spruce treated the grunts with respect and often visited with the enlisted Marines in the trenches, and is remembered as having been a genuine friend.

Other close friends, who Dan remembers only by their nicknames, included Chief, a Native American from the Midwest who bucked the stereotype of an immature, rowdy Marine by always exhibiting common sense, and Professor, a well-spoken, low-key bookworm, and one of the few grunts Dan would meet who was a college graduate. J.R. Garcia, a Californian of Mexican decent, was famous for turning C-rations into four-star meals, a byproduct of his mother being employed in a menial job at a factory that produced the ready-to-eat meals.

Speaking of food, another friend was Roland "Pee Wee" Dean, probably the biggest Marine, physically speaking, in the whole company, who ate as much food as he could possibly get his hands on. One of Dan's closest friends was "Crazy" Steve Nichols, who had the courage to do almost anything, and could use his gift of gab to sell a bridge to nowhere. Ironically, Steve was from Philadelphia and grew up in the same neighborhood as Dan, but because Dan had been enrolled at Catholic school and Steve had attended public school, the two never met until serving together in Vietnam.

Other friends included Lance Hayduke, a stereotypical surfer-dude from California, with bleach-blond hair, blue eyes, and a love of the Beach Boys, and John Abbey, an excitable guy from McKeesport, Pennsylvania, who enjoyed teasing Dan about the way he pronounced the word water (Philadelphians tend to pronounce it "wooder"). Jake Tatum, a tough as nails, poster-boy Marine, who at twenty had already served several tours of duty in Vietnam, was also a close friend, in part because he took newer recruits under his wing until they became more accustomed to life in Vietnam. Tatum's physical opposite was Ralph "Papa" Pappas, a skinny, awkward looking Marine who Dan never though fit into the Marine Corps mold, but was still very likeable. And there was "Stein-man" Steinmetz, a married twenty-year-old from Seattle, Washington.

There were many other friends, too. Some names have faded from memory due to the passage of time. Others, with whom Dan became acquainted, did not live long enough for him to really get a chance to know. Dan often wondered if they were the lucky ones. He never wanted anyone to die, but he reasoned that if it was destined to happen, better it should occur sooner rather than later in a tour. At least if death came sooner, the suffering associated with the abomination of the war was minimized.

Ultimately, Dan considered all the Marines beside whom he fought in Vietnam to be his friends. Some died on the field of battle. Others had the good fortune to make it home in one piece. Others were less fortunate, and returned with debilitating injuries. Of all his memories from the war, Dan's fondest are of his friends. To this day, they all remain in his thoughts.

Fishing With Hand Grenades

Marines of Charlie Company 1/26 at Khe Sanh, as photographed by David Douglas Duncan. First published in *Life Magazine*, February 23, 1968. (Reproduced with permission.)

Chapter 10

-Payback-

"The first casualty when war comes is the truth."
                                    -U.S. Senator Hiram Johnson

March 26, 1968
Journal Entry

I am sitting here right now feeling numb. To be honest, I have not been well since Robbie died. It's so hard to believe he is gone. The most difficult part is that I have all this grief and anger bottled up inside of me, and there is nothing I can do about it. There is no way to vent, no one to whom to talk. All of my feelings just fester in my gut, building up until I think they are going to explode inside of me. I want to go out there and get some payback from those motherfuckers who killed Robbie. But I can't. Not yet.

March 29, 1968
Journal Entry

One of the toughest things to accept about our situation is that we have been held in a defensive position for such a long time. Instead of being able to move outside the perimeter and actively engage the enemy, we have to sit on our butts all day and do nothing. We are stuck in these damn trenches with no other choice but to absorb the constant pounding from the NVA incoming, and it is driving us crazy. Each of us is itching for the opportunity to push out and get some retribution for all the Marines who have already been killed. During the last two months, we've watched our friends die without being allowed to fight back, and now it's time for those of us who remain to take the initiative. We've been told that tomorrow we're finally going to have our chance.

An attack has been planned on a heavily fortified NVA position close to the base perimeter, very near the area where the twenty-five Marines from Bravo Company were ambushed and killed on February

25. Their bodies were never recovered, and we assume that they are still lying out on the field of battle, rotting away. One of the mottoes of the Marine Corps is that we never leave our dead behind, and Marines at Khe Sanh aren't about to stop following tradition. It's only right that since those who were killed back in February were from 1/26, Marines from 1/26 will get to lead the assault to retrieve the bodies.

It feels like forever that we have been waiting for an occasion to recover the bodies of the guys who were ambushed. Actually, though, this will be just as much a payback mission as it is a search and recovery operation. This is our opportunity to let go of ten weeks of anger and hostility that has been building up inside of us. Our aim is to kick some ass when we move out tomorrow morning.

March 30, 1968
It was still dark when Dan awoke on the morning of March 30. He calmly began to prepare for the day's action by having a small bite to eat, and then thoroughly inspecting his weapons and gear and double-checking that he would be carrying plenty of ammunition. As 0600 approached, Marines from Bravo and Charlie Company formed up and began making their way to the far end of the base runway. While an entire Marine company would have otherwise presented an inviting target for NVA snipers, the fog was extremely dense this morning, providing them plenty of cover.

On its orders, Dan's platoon moved forward, penetrating several hundred yards into the jungle. The tension hung as thick as the fog. Everyone knew what was awaiting them, and that it was only a matter of time before they would come across the NVA. As he walked, Dan imagined he was hearing the rapidly beating hearts of those around him. Or, it occurred to him, maybe his mind was just overloaded with the thunderous beats coming from his own chest.

About a half-hour after departing the base, 2nd Platoon reached its first checkpoint. Everyone dropped to their stomachs and waited for orders on how to proceed. Dan glanced around anxiously. The base had disappeared from view, obscured by fog and ground cover. Eli Hanks kneeled only a couple of yards away, quietly talking with the base over the radio. He finished checking off his coordinates and swiftly hung up the receiver.

As the minutes unfolded, Dan remained motionless on the ground. He was nervous yet excited, and determined to fight capably. Spooked by a noise, he looked to his left and observed Rodriguez fastening a bayonet to his M-16. Dan and several other Marines began to follow suit. As Dan affixed his bayonet to his rifle, he caught sight of the end of the blade. The tip of the blade was missing and, noticing this, his thoughts immediately turned to Robbie. Dan reflected on how the tip was broken off prior to the start of the siege, when he and Robbie were roughhousing. In addition to breaking the bayonet, they had also ended up spilling a drum of water, which even then had been a precious commodity. Dan recalled how he and Robbie laughed uncontrollably under their breath, while a hotheaded officer who witnessed their antics reprimanded them for their carelessness. In spite of the fear he now felt, Dan managed to smile to himself at the memory. Securing the blade tightly, Dan presumed that a broken bayonet was better than none at all.

For the next twenty minutes, the platoon remained at rest, enveloped by the intense fog. A sergeant Dan had never seen before today crawled over to the radio, picked up the receiver, and talked for a minute or two. When he hung up, he turned to address the Marines.

"Everyone, listen up," he screamed in a hushed tone across the line. "Time for some fucking payback. We're gonna get up on-line and begin to advance forward. If you see something move, you kill it."

The Marines, to this point, had done an adept job of using the heavy fog to their advantage. So proficient had they been that they had unknowingly advanced to within yards of a heavily fortified trench and bunker system occupied by an entire NVA battalion.

In near perfect unison, the Marines stood up and began moving forward.

1/26 Marines Command Chronology

```
    At  0800  B-3  started  taking  mortars,  small
arms  fire  and  automatic  weapons  fire  from  a
fortified  position  to  their  direct  front.  B-1
and  B-3  commenced  the  assault  on  the  fortified
positions   utilizing   small   arms,   grenades,
flamethrowers and demo charges.
```

Fishing With Hand Grenades

March 30, 1968
Journal Entry

. . . and then the distinct poof of a mortar sounded. Seconds later, a barrage of NVA mortars landed only yards from our position, exploding violently. We returned fire as best we could while slowly advancing. The NVA, who were now right in front of us, fired back. As soon as the NVA small arms fire started, we broke loose from our line and charged into the North Vietnamese line, shooting at anything we saw. Gunfire rattled off in every direction, and smoke filled the air. The fighting was bitter, and wounded and dead bodies began to litter the ground.

I fought forward, repeating over and over the process of emptying my clip and reloading. We got so close to the NVA that guys found themselves engaging in hand-to-hand combat. Marines started attacking enemy soldiers with bayonets, entrenching tools, helmets, or any other makeshift weapons they could devise. I saw someone bashing in the head of an NVA soldier with the butt of a rifle. It was gruesome.

At some point, a grenade exploded to my left. I was struck by shrapnel and fell to the ground, more out of instinct than pain. Robinson, who was fighting next to me, was closer to the grenade when it exploded, and he went down with a scream. Even from where I was lying on the ground, I could tell that he was injured badly.

I paused for a second to take inventory of myself. Being hit with shrapnel felt like having someone throw a tiny handful of burning hot pebbles at you at an extremely high velocity. It hurt, but the shock was not paralyzing. My primary interest was in checking to see where I had been hit. The wounds were mostly in my arm. My sleeve was ripped and bloody, but I had so much adrenaline running through me that I barely noticed any pain.

I could hear Robinson moaning, and looked over to see that the doc had already gotten to him. Concluding he was in good hands, I rolled onto my belly and began inching forward again. I kept firing and reloading, making sure to stay as low to the ground as I could.

Our M-60 gunners, who were just a few feet down the line from me, kept putting out hundreds of rounds at a time and never seemed to let up. I was lucky they were nearby, in the sense that when I finally reached the NVA trenches, nearly all the enemy I encountered were already dead. For two hours, we swept through the trenches, mopping up anything that wasn't a Marine. Finally, the call came.

"Cease fire! Cease fire!"

For a moment, I had a sense of déjà vu. As was the case on February 25, the fighting was marked by nearly total confusion and an enormous amount of bloodshed. On this occasion, however, the NVA were the ones on the receiving end. For now, we had convincingly turned the tables.

The firefight over, I stood still and looked around. The air stunk of gunpowder. There was nothing more to kill. I noticed the large number of bodies sprawled about, and I suddenly turned sick to my stomach. My body began to hurt. The skin on my arm where I was hit by shrapnel felt like it was on fire. My hands and arms were sticky with blood. I could hear my heart pounding in my chest. Marines and NVA alike moaned in pain from wounds caused by gunshots and grenades that hadn't finished the job. This was all so idiotic, I thought to myself. What a stupid fucking waste this really was.

—

The casualties from the hostilities on the morning of March 30 were extensive. The North Vietnamese body count reached 115, and the Marines suffered nine dead with another seventy-one wounded.[1] Included among the US wounded was Dan, who suffered injuries to his arms caused by grenade shrapnel.

—

Although clearly not the decisive battle for the base, what the grunts termed "payback" represented a turning point in the defense of Khe Sanh. After two-and-a-half months, the siege of the combat base was now all but over. A large portion of the North Vietnamese who had surrounded the area either were dead or had retreated. The Marines had officially succeeded in holding onto Khe Sanh. Operation Scotland, which commenced on November 1, 1967, ended on March 31, 1968.[2]

Official Marine records for Operation Scotland list 205 friendly killed in action and 816 friendly wounded. These casualty figures, which include not only the eleven weeks of the siege (officially January 21 to April 6), but also the preceding eleven weeks, are not universally accepted as accurate or candid.[3]

Fishing With Hand Grenades

Dan's personal recollection was that a day would never pass without Marines being killed in action at Khe Sanh. On the two or three occasions he found himself at Graves Registration, he observed body bags stacked one on top of the other, more lifeless bodies to be flown back to the States. While he never took a count of all the dead Marines that he saw, he strongly believes that there were many more than 205 killed. And by Dan's account, this was only what he observed in his own battalion. There were three other Marine battalions at Khe Sanh, and in his mind, it is reasonable to conclude that they each suffered a similar number of casualties. Even if one took a very conservative approach and assumed that each battalion, manned with approximately 1,000 soldiers, suffered one casualty every day of the eleven-week siege, then approximately 300 Marine personnel, or nearly 50% more than the official figure of 205, would have given their lives in the defense of the base.

Curiously, the military chaplain who served at Khe Sanh estimated that 475 Marines were killed in January, February, and March alone.[4] It could be argued that this is the most realistic estimate of the correct casualty number, because the chaplain's duties included presiding over last rites and presume objectivity.

Regardless, the official totals of 205 killed and 816 wounded do not include any of the numerous personnel from other military branches who died when the planes and helicopters in which they were flying crash-landed at Khe Sanh under heavy anti-aircraft fire. While understandable that these numbers are not relevant to the Marine casualty figures, they also fail to show up in any other official Khe Sanh casualty report. Shouldn't the brave airmen who sacrificed their lives also be included among those killed in defense of the base?

Is it fair then to suggest that the official Marine record of 205 Marines killed in action at Khe Sanh was, in actuality, too low? Furthermore, is it possible that the number of killed in action was intentionally underestimated or undercounted? Would the US military have reason to purposefully understate the body count regarding the American Marines whose lives were lost at Khe Sanh? Many, including Dan, believe the answer to all three of these questions is "yes."

Although General William Westmoreland termed body counts "the whipping boy of the press," a commander of India Company 3/26 may have summed it up best when he said, "Most body counts were pure and unadulterated bull-shit. Generals manipulated a 'good kill' by flip-flopping numbers."[5]

Body counts were widely believed to be numbers used to appease both the American press, and perhaps more importantly, the American public.[6] To that end, body counts soon became the statistic through which military success or failure was measured, by both American troops and the community at large back home. The numbers became the yardstick used to gauge the battlefield.[7]

How did this scenario play out? By manipulating body counts, American military commanders may have hoped to create the appearance of success in a war that was slowly slipping through their fingers. In 1968, as the war intensified and the siege of Khe Sanh was lifted, American opposition to the conflict grew more vocal. Often, the high death toll of American soldiers provided fuel for the protesters' fires. Given the focus and attention Khe Sanh received in the American press, and if the true number of casualties was actually considerably higher than 205, then certainly those in charge could have been motivated to manipulate the body counts at Khe Sanh. It is very possible that the US military perceived the circulation of this type of misleading information as a means of downplaying what, in essence, had amounted to a military public relations disaster.

In the final analysis, one could reasonably argue that even if the record keepers were not explicitly demeaning the sacrifice of our fighters at Khe Sanh, the military most certainly left the impression with those who fought there that the lives lost at Khe Sanh could be chalked up as worthy of something less than full recognition. For Dan, it was as though the military commanders were unwilling to exhibit even the most basic respect for the soldiers who battled and died at the base. Why else then would the military, in citing casualties at Khe Sanh, fail to acknowledge the ultimate sacrifice of every member of the US armed forces who gave his life in connection with the defense of the combat base?

♠

Chapter 11

-Khe Sanh, After the Siege-

"I have just returned from visiting the Marines at the front, and there is not a finer fighting organization in the world."
-General Douglas MacArthur

On April 1, 1968, Operation Pegasus commenced. The objectives of the operation were to open Route 9, relieve the Khe Sanh Combat Base, and kill off any remaining NVA contingents in the area.[1] For the next six days, 30,000 troops from the 1st and 3rd Marines trudged down Route 9, with the 1st Army Air Calvary leading the way.[2]

—

Dan's attention was drawn toward the sky to the south. He had been told that the Army was planning to relieve Khe Sanh. Hearing this news, he envisioned a convoy of troops approaching the base in a scene reminiscent of a D-day-style invasion. But what he observed in the distance was a sight beyond anything he could have pictured. Black dots covered the horizon, giving the appearance of a swarm of locusts blanketing the heavens. However, what was unfurling before Dan was not the panorama of a biblical plague, but hundreds of helicopters filling the sky as far as his eyes could see. The mass of helicopters descending upon Khe Sanh was ferrying troops who would relieve the wearied and battered Marines, now valiantly defending the base since January.

—

Shortly after the Army began to reopen Route 9, Dan was flown to Phu Bai to receive medical treatment for the injuries he sustained days earlier during payback. Having suffered shrapnel wounds on his arms, legs, and stomach, he would require a short hospital stay.

April 4, 1968
As if their worlds were not already turbulent enough, the wounded Marines who sat around the hospital's television set were about to be rocked by another blast of bad news. The voice of the television re-

porter was filled with grief and disbelief as he spoke solemnly into the camera.

"Once again, we are receiving unconfirmed reports that civil rights leader Dr. Martin Luther King Jr. has been assassinated."

The hospital rec room had fallen deafly quiet. The chatter that usually hummed through the room had been muted by the shocking news. The mix of white, black, and Hispanic soldiers, many dressed in bandages and confined to wheel chairs, listened in a state of stunned silence as the news of Dr. King's death reached them halfway around the world.

That evening, while resting in the hospital dormitory, Dan overheard conversations in which white soldiers nervously expressed worry about problems they might encounter with black soldiers now that word had circulated that a white man had allegedly killed Dr. King. Although he could understand the basis for the anxiety, Dan was not concerned about the calamity creating difficulties for him. He would soon be back at Khe Sanh, and in his outfit, race was simply not a subject of contention. The old saying, "There are no atheists in foxholes," was, in Dan's mind, as applicable to racists as to atheists. Having spent months in a unit composed of whites, blacks, Hispanics, and Native Americans, Dan could not recall a single racially charged incident. In his unit, there were always more important matters to focus upon than race. Most guys were too busy concentrating on getting home alive to pay attention to the color of someone's skin. Words like nigger, spic, or kike were never uttered. If someone was considered an asshole, race or religion did not factor into the equation. An asshole was an asshole, plain and simple. Skin color or a person's religious faith or ethnicity was never an issue, perhaps because in the end, none of that mattered when it came time to take a bullet or save a life.

April 8, 1968

Dear Mom,

Well, I am sorry to report that I have returned to Khe Sanh. After a few days of having my wounds tended to in Phu Bai, I was ordered back to the base on the 5th to rejoin my unit. The good news is that the siege is now over, and the incoming has stopped completely. It almost seems like a dream come true. No longer do we have to live in the dirt with the rats, and there's no more constant fear of dying.

I barely remembered what it had been like to live as a normal human being. To help remind me of what life was like here before the siege, I took a walk around the base the day I returned, and it was such a great feeling to be in the open without worrying about being killed. It almost seemed as though the war was over, although I knew it really wasn't. At least for the moment, however, the bloodshed has ended for those of us at Khe Sanh.

Yesterday, my platoon left the base on foot and headed north into the nearby hills. We had orders to secure the region around the base, conduct sweeps of the immediate surroundings, and to look for any remaining signs of enemy activity. We ran into bunker complexes and trench systems, and found some evidence of NVA staging areas, but other than that, there isn't much left to identify. That's because most of the area surrounding the base was totally destroyed, especially where the B-52s dropped their bombs.

Of everything we came across, nothing left me more awestruck than walking through sites where arc lights had dropped their payloads. The bombs left craters measuring about fifty feet across, and deep enough that if a grown man stood in the center and it filled with water, the water would easily rise over his head. I saw some holes in the ground that were literally as big as houses. And of course, in the vicinity of the craters there was complete devastation. We would find body parts and small remnants of military equipment, but not much more. There might be blood and guts, like a finger or an arm, maybe even a leg or head, but rarely any whole bodies.

One of the craziest things we ran into near one of the craters was a torso with no arms, legs, or head. It was horrifying to look at, but at the same time, I couldn't take my eyes off it. Something else I saw that really freaked me out was the corpse of an NVA soldier who had apparently died from a napalm attack. Half of his body was burned and grossly disfigured, while the other half was somehow untouched. It was a very odd sight, and reminded me of a half-man, half-woman carnival sideshow performer. . . .

Love,
Daniel

April 10, 1968

With no large-scale violence occurring since the end of the siege, and the last several days having been especially quiet, the Marines were starting to become less tense, the overwhelming stress of the past three months finally beginning to loosen its grip. There was some hope that a major turning point in the war had occurred. Praying that the lull would continue and they would encounter no significant combat, Dan's unit dug into fighting positions on a hill northeast of the base and settled in for the night. By now, Dan's unit was spending more time off the base than on it, and while their excursions into the hills had been relatively uneventful to date, this positive development brought little comfort to the Marines.

As the stars began to appear in the evening sky, Dan sat on the edge of a freshly dug trench with Rodriguez, Billy Chamberlain, and Steve Nichols, listening to music on a transistor radio and reminiscing about Robbie. Their camp was positioned on the hill above a steep slope, which had taken quite some time and effort to climb earlier in the day. The Marines relaxed, smoking cigarettes and joking around, convinced they were immune from a ground attack because the landscape would present too challenging a climb for the NVA. The song "South Street" began playing on the radio, and Dan's thoughts shifted from Robbie to distant memories of home. He missed Philadelphia, and looked forward to his return with great anticipation.

Suddenly, the calm of the night was shattered by shots fired at the base of the hill on which they were positioned. The Marines turned in the direction of the shots and observed sparks flying into the air. They knew immediately that they were under attack.

As the Marines would later learn, when the evening's listening post was dispatched at dusk to keep watch on the hill's perimeter, the LP stumbled into an area where some NVA units surrounding the hill were preparing to conduct a raid to be launched later that night. Surprised by the approach of the LP, the NVA commenced its assault ahead of schedule. The LP was ambushed and its members shot dead, almost at point blank range.

As the NVA attack got underway, mortars pummeled the hill, and AK-47 fire started hitting the Marines' positions, catching them off-guard. Fearing for their lives, Dan and Steve bounded toward the nearest fighting hole. The opening they located was dug out to fit only two people, but when Dan and Steve jumped in, they discovered Ralph Pappas and Billy Lee already squatting on the floor. Rather than expose themselves to enemy fire by climbing out and moving to another location, Dan and Steve chose instead to squeeze into the undersized foxhole. From their cramped quarters, they spent the rest of the night battling for their lives with no room to maneuver. Billy and Ralph could do little more than stay on the bottom of the hole and feed magazines to Dan and Steve.

The evening's encounter was bloody and heated, and it took the Marines many hours to repel the NVA attack. Several Marines were killed, including the platoon's M-60 gunner, who was positioned in the next hole over. Dan was horrified as he watched the gunner take a direct hit to the chest from a rocket-propelled grenade, the force of which seemingly blew him to pieces, right before Dan's eyes.

April 12, 1968

It was early in the evening of Good Friday. Dan's unit was situated on top of one of the numerous and indistinguishable hills surrounding Khe Sanh. This marked their sixth different nighttime position in as many days. The particular hill on which they were dug in was connected by a narrow ridge of land to an adjacent hill, which was occupied by another Marine platoon. That night, Dan's unit became engaged in a firefight with an NVA probe, and requested a supporting artillery barrage from the combat base. Unfortunately, due most likely to the chaos generated by the firefight, the artillery gunner firing from the base used incorrect coordinates in aiming at his target. Instead of hitting the NVA position at the base of the hill, the artillery rounds made a direct hit on the adjacent hill where the other Marine platoon was positioned. As a consequence, several Marines were killed by friendly fire, and others were severely burned by the searing hot, white phosphorous rounds.

Shortly after the friendly fire incident, heavy North Vietnamese rocket fire pounded Dan's platoon, which encircled the crown of the hill. Dan's position on the south side of the hill was spared from the attack, inasmuch as the NVA were firing from the north side, and the peak of the hill provided a natural defense against the rockets. When the rocket volleys ended, Dan and several others worked their way to the north side of the hill to search for wounded companions.

What they discovered was disheartening. Lying on the ground were several Marines, their remains covered with blood and disfigured. One body in particular was strikingly horrific. While the others were bloodied and suffered open wounds, one Marine had no visible injuries, not even a single scratch. Instead, he was totally contorted and twisted, like a giant pretzel. It was as if his every bone was transformed to jelly. Dan surmised that one of the rockets had impacted far enough away so as not to cause a direct hit upon the Marine, but close enough so that the concussion of the explosion turned his body into human silly putty.

April 14, 1968
Journal Entry

Yesterday morning, while our unit conducted a sweep in front of one of the many hills we have been relegated to guarding, we got into some shit with North Vietnamese forces. Even though there is no longer an official "NVA siege" in the Khe Sanh area, this last week we have found ourselves increasingly engaged in small skirmishes. I guess there are still random enemy units that have not received word that the battle is over. Anyway, a couple of our guys were shot when the NVA jumped us, but fortunately no one was killed. The whole incident was actually over pretty quickly, lasting less than a minute. There were just a few NVA that opened up on us, and when they did, our entire platoon returned fire. I emptied my magazine, and before there was time to reload, we had put them down.

That same day, in the afternoon, we received orders to once again take a nighttime position on top of yet another hill. We arrived at the base of the hill later in the day than planned, and some of our guys were nervous about darkness setting in before securing the summit. They were afraid it would prove too dangerous to complete the operation in the dark, because there might be NVA still lingering in the vicinity. As the distant sky glowed purple and orange, we double-timed it up the steep, ragged incline, and reached the peak before the sun completely set. We had cleared the area and secured our position just in time, but we still needed to build our nighttime entrenchments.

Exhausted from our climb, Rodriguez and I worked as best we could with the little light we had, digging ourselves a deep fighting hole. After more than an hour of physical exertion, we were worn out, and started taking shifts on watch so that we could both get some sleep.

The plan was for us to rotate, with one of us sleeping for two hours while the other stayed on alert. It was about 0400, and I was just beginning my third turn on watch when I noticed a strange shape in front of our position. Initially, I thought it might be someone sneaking up on us. The longer I stared, however, the more obvious it became that whatever it was wasn't moving. Still, the uncertainty of the situation drove me to remain on guard. Using my right hand, I kept my gun aimed at whatever was there, and with my left hand, I controlled the detonator for a claymore mine that we had buried in front of our hole.

As daylight started to appear over the horizon, the object in front of me began to take form. Finally, there was enough light to clearly make it out, and the realization of what I was looking at nearly took my breath away. In the darkness of last evening, and in our rush to establish our fighting position as quickly as possible, Rodriguez and I had failed to notice the danger lurking in our immediate surroundings. Now, however, with the benefit of sufficient light, I could easily recognize the tail fin of a 500-pound bomb protruding from the ground, just like the tip of an iceberg sticks out from the surface of water. The bomb, which was not more than ten yards away, had been dropped, probably from a Phantom, during one of the many air strikes associated with the siege, and had somehow failed to detonate. Regardless, as I stared at it, I had every reason to believe that it was still a very live round.

When I realized that we were sitting in front of a live bomb containing enough explosive power to kill every member of the platoon, I woke Rodriguez, and we immediately ran to another hole as far away from the bomb as we could get. Later, I sat reflecting on the likelihood that if I had shot at the bomb in the dark or popped the claymore, judging that the fin was an enemy soldier, I could have very easily detonated the bomb and blown up the entire hillside.

April 17, 1968

Dear Mom,

Happy belated Easter. I wish that I could have been there to enjoy Easter dinner with you and the rest of the family, but that will have to wait until next year. I do have something exciting to report to you, though. On the 15th, the day after Easter, my unit returned to the combat base and found out that we would be leaving Khe Sanh for good. It was the best news I've heard in a long time.

The following morning, as I caught sight of a Marine squad preparing to head out into the jungle, my unit eagerly boarded choppers assigned to take us far away from Khe Sanh. With the last Marine on board, the choppers took to the air and started circling the base to gain altitude. As wind whipped through the deck, I looked out the open door of the chopper, onto the base below, and began to think about how happy I was to be leaving. It was not lost on me that I would never again have to see that godforsaken place.

Gazing down on the base, the difference between how it now looked as compared to the day I first arrived was as distinct as the contrast between black and white. When I first flew into Khe Sanh, the neighboring valleys and plateaus had been covered with lush vegetation and surrounded by beautifully foliated hills. I distinctly remember how impressed I was with how green everything was. But now there was nothing. Everything was blown up and torn from the ground. The landscape was scorched. Virtually no vegetation remained. All the buildings that had stood when I came here were also gone, replaced instead with underground facilities that were hardly noticeable from the sky. Destruction and reminders of death were everywhere. For as far as the eye could see, everything had been burned, bombed, and shot apart. Khe Sanh was completely ravaged.

As I continued reflecting upon my experiences at the base and the past months of hardships, my joy over our departure turned bittersweet. Yes, Khe Sanh had been a living hell for me since January. I had lived for weeks on end in the filthy, sodden, rat-infested earth. I was always hungry, surviving on meager rations of food and water. I had escaped death every day by fighting and praying for survival. Unquestionably, it was the worst period of my life.

On the other hand, there were the countless memories of friends to whom I was saying goodbye, many of whom had shed blood into the ground below. As I watched the base growing smaller beneath me, imagining the bloodstained soil, it felt as if I was leaving a part of those guys behind. They teach us to never leave a soldier behind. Well, I lost many friends at Khe Sanh, and it is hard to move on without them. The memories of the friendships made and lost at Khe Sanh are something that I know I will never forget. . . .

Love,
Daniel

—

By April 6, the siege of Khe Sanh had officially become a part of history. For seventy-seven days, the world watched as 6,000 Marines defended the base and absorbed the continual barrage of North Vietnamese incoming that rained down upon them. After two-and-a-half months of fighting, Khe Sanh ranked as one of the fiercest, deadliest, and most highly contested sieges in the history of warfare. The sheer numbers of casualties alone reflected the horror of the battle. Thousands of enemy soldiers were killed, and thousands upon thousands injured. Although the true number will probably never be known, it was estimated that as many as 15,000 NVA were killed in the attempt to gain control of Khe Sanh.[3]

When all was said and done, Vo Nguyen Giap never realized his dream of accomplishing another Dien Bien Phu. The Marines were successful in their defense of the Khe Sanh Combat Base, notwithstanding that they were susceptible to being easily overrun. In terms of battlefield strategy, Giap had the Marines at Khe Sanh right where he wanted them. American reinforcements were light and sporadic, supplies were low, and the Marines were outnumbered almost 7 to 1. But the North ultimately failed in its attempt to capture the base for three primary reasons.

The first of these reasons was the incredible firepower of the Americans. While the NVA shelled the combat base daily, the Americans answered with a substantial amount of shelling in their own right. During the siege, the allies fired a remarkable 192,081 rounds of artillery in defense of the base. The Americans also flew a total of 2,700 arc lights and another 24,000 tactical air sorties.[4] In all, over 110,000 tons of bombs were dropped during the seventy-seven-day siege of Khe Sanh.[5] Put in another context, that tonnage represented 5,700 five hundred-pound bombs per day! It was by far the most concentrated bombardment by aircraft that had ever taken place during any battle in history. This endless barrage of B-52 and tactical air sorties wiped out large numbers of NVA soldiers, along with their entrenchments and supplies. The French had never come close to matching this type of response against their adversaries at Dien Bien Phu. In addition to the fire support, while supplies always seemed few and far between, the military still managed to deliver over 17,000 tons of supplies by air to the base during the course of the siege.[6] To put that quantity into perspective, it translates into more than 5,500 pounds of food, water, clothing, and ammunition for each Marine stationed on the base.

The second explanation for the North's failure to seize Khe Sanh was the nature of the terrain near the base. The geographic features of the surrounding area drew comparisons to Dien Bien Phu, but the topography of the ground immediately surrounding Khe Sanh made a full offensive assault much more difficult to achieve than had been the case against the French. In order to approach the base at Khe Sanh, the NVA soldiers needed to maneuver downhill, through unstable ground, then traverse steep-sided ravines, and lastly climb up to the plateau on which the base was situated. Of course, all this had to be accomplished in the face of heavy artillery, small arms fire, and air strikes.

But the most important reason behind the North's defeat was the will of the Marines who defended Khe Sanh. It came down to the courage, strength, and determination of the foot soldiers who lived in the trenches of Khe Sanh, who slept in their own shit and piss, and who endured seventy-seven consecutive days of hell while watching, often helplessly, as their close friends were killed and wounded. The resolve and determination of those in the trenches to survive made it possible for the defenders of Khe Sanh to prevail. No military rhetoric about the role of the military planners' skill and leadership could ever obscure the truth of the matter. The deciding factor in keeping the combat base out of the hands of the North was not the generals and colonels, but the spirit that resided in the hearts and minds of the grunts who served in the infantry during the siege of Khe Sanh.

Chapter 12

-A Shau Valley/Operation Delaware-

"What doesn't kill you, only makes you stronger."
-Frederich Nietzche

April 17, 1968
1/26 Marines Command Chronology
   Summary of Periods Action: 1st Battalion 26th Marines moved from Khe Sanh to Wonder Beach.

April 18, 1968

Dear Mom,
   Well, I finally get to write you from my new home. After leaving Khe Sanh aboard helicopters, we were flown to an Army base in Quang Tri Province. Once we arrived, all of 1st Battalion was assembled, and a memorial service was held for those killed at Khe Sanh. A chaplain read some prayers and gave an unremarkable speech, which was followed by a twenty-one-gun salute and the playing of "taps." I stood at attention through the entire ceremony, dwelling on Robbie and my other departed friends. I wondered if this was all the military thought of so many lost lives—a couple of prayers and a few rifle salutes. It made me furious to think about the needless killing that had occurred. The longer I reflected on it, the more my anger turned to sadness. I didn't want to end up breaking down in front of the entire battalion, so by the end of the ceremony I was trying to divert my thoughts to anything else I could bring to mind.
   Afterwards, the Army officially welcomed us. We were told that we would be getting hot food and showers, and issued new clothing and gear. We were so excited about the news, you would have thought we were children opening presents on Christmas morning. Even though I was fortunate enough to get out of Khe Sanh once during the siege, and then once after payback, others had endured the entire siege without a

break. For those Marines, it would be the first time in nearly three months that they would enjoy such luxuries.

We took our showers with hot water and soap, and received all new clothing and gear. It felt incredible to put on a fresh cotton tee shirt that was not covered in dirt and blood, and did not smell to high-hell from having been worn for weeks on end. Next, we went to the mess tent and had ourselves a gigantic feast. There would be no C-rations at this meal. We ate nothing but freshly made food. As with the showers and new clothing, for some, it was the first hot meal in months. We devoured trays of steak and mashed potatoes, gravy, vegetables, fresh bread, and tons of water and juice. The food was delicious. It was one of the greatest meals I've ever eaten.

Unfortunately, all that terrific food didn't continue for very long. At lunch this afternoon, a big fight broke out in the mess tent between the Army and the Marines. It started as a rowdy food fight, but eventually guys were jumping across tables, throwing punches, and getting into fistfights. Even though the Army grunts were equally responsible for what happened, they blamed the Marines for starting the incident, and as a result, we're no longer allowed into the mess facility for meals. So, at least for now, we're back to eating C-rations. To tell you the truth, I really don't care. I'm just content having made it this far and being able to eat at all. . . .

Love,
Daniel

April 19, 1968
Journal Entry

This place is unbelievable. At least for the time being, there are no LPs, patrols, or ambushes to carry out. For that matter, there is nothing else for us to do that would require leaving the base, firing our guns, or could otherwise result in any of us being killed. Our unit's only orders are to provide security for a sector of the base, which is something my sister Emily could do. It basically amounts to little more than bunker watch. The best part about our duty here is that the line for which our unit is responsible ends at the ocean, so all we've been doing is hanging out on the beach.

The ocean is absolutely beautiful. It's nothing like the Jersey shore. The sand is pearly white, the water is clear blue, and at night, when the moon shines down on the water, everything seems to magically sparkle. In the evenings, we go hang out at the beach, drink beer, smoke, and swim in the ocean. The coolest thing about swimming in the ocean is that these little green, algae-like organisms cling to our bodies, and as the moon shines down, the algae, or whatever it is, becomes illuminated and sparkles like tiny green sequins. I know this might not seem like much to get excited about, but right now, even the little things in this world are special. You definitely gain a greater appreciation for all that life has to offer after near-death experiences. And I would certainly qualify Khe Sanh as a near-death experience.

Even though we are still serving in the infantry, I'm not worried about being shot while here, and there is no fucking incoming from which we must hide. I'm happy just to be alive, plus this gig is better than I could have ever imagined. There are even some local girls who frequent the base and have decided that they like hanging out with the Marines better than the Army. I sure can't complain about this assignment.

April 20, 1968

Dan sat by himself, gazing out at the endless ocean, feeling the cool sand envelop his feet as he dug them into the ground. The moon was nearly full tonight, and it hung low in the distant sky. In one hand, he held a cold beer, in the other a lit cigarette. A small fire, which someone had started with some old crates, crackled nearby. Other Marines in his unit were enjoying themselves swimming in the ocean and roughhousing on the beach.

"Hey, Dan," Steve shouted from the water's edge. "Come on in. The water's great."

"In a second, man," Dan responded.

For the moment, Dan just wanted to be by himself and reflect on the past months. Try as he might, he could not shake his memories of Khe Sanh. Dan knew he should begin to put the experience behind him and move forward, but doing so was proving next to impossible. There were so many memories in his head that he couldn't dislodge, on top of which he wasn't exactly looking toward the future with great enthusiasm. Certainly, there were more horrors awaiting him the next time he went into the bush. Dan knew beach duty wasn't going to last forever. He survived Khe Sanh, but the war wasn't over, and he still had several months left on his tour. It just didn't seem fair that although he had made it out of Khe Sanh alive, there was probably much more tough combat ahead. Hadn't he already been through enough? It was a question other members of his unit were beginning to ask out loud.

"Hey, Dan." It was Alonzo trying to get his attention. "Want another beer?"

Dan held his can, still half-full and slightly cold, into the air, and shook his head.

"No, thanks, man. I'm fine."

Dan took another drag from his smoke. He missed Robbie. It was hard being around everyone and not having Robbie's company.

"Son of a bitch," Dan angrily exclaimed under his breath. "Robbie, man, why the fuck did you die?" he grumbled bitterly.

He shook the thought from his head and tried to focus on more upbeat images. As he took a deep drag on his cigarette, Dan became engrossed in the glow of the moon glistening on the surface of the ocean. It all looked so peaceful and tranquil. Dan wanted to believe the worst was over, even as worrisome thoughts of the future crept to the forefront of his mind. He took a big gulp of his beer, put out his smoke in the sand, and headed over to join his friends in the water.

—

As the war continued, there were few places in South Vietnam where the NVA could operate with freedom of movement and in relative safety. One area where the NVA could act with impunity was in A Shau Valley.[1] The valley was a twenty-five-mile-long stretch of land that lay thirty miles southwest of Hue and forty miles southeast of Khe Sanh, with the most westerly part of the valley stretching into Laos.[2] A Shau stood completely surrounded by 5,000-foot peaks that were covered with jungle canopy. The valley floor was blanketed by six-foot-high elephant grass, interspersed with tropical rain forests.[3]

In light of its strategic location and the dense cover it provided, A Shau became a prominent NVA staging area and a key infiltration route from Laos via the Ho Chi Minh trail. The NVA used the trail, which was actually comprised of an elaborate system of numerous jungle trails, for smuggling supplies into the South, especially into the cities of Hue and Da Nang. Besides serving as a haven for smugglers, the hills of A Shau were fortified by NVA anti-aircraft guns capable of hitting planes flying at altitudes of over 20,000 feet.[4] For these reasons, maintaining control of A Shau became a top priority for the North.

During much of the year, the weather in A Shau did not favor American military movements, allowing the NVA to operate within the valley virtually undisturbed. In April and May, however, the weather cleared up sufficiently to allow the Americans to initiate offensive operations. The timing of the lifting of the siege at Khe Sanh, in conjunction with improved weather, provided a perfect opportunity to undertake Operation Delaware. This action was to involve a combination of Army, Marine, and ARVN forces that would attack NVA contingents in the valley in an attempt to interdict supply routes and flush enemy troops from the area. With the siege of Khe Sanh ended, the US military was able to direct sufficient manpower and other resources in support of Operation Delaware, thus taking advantage of the narrow window of opportunity afforded by the lull in the weather.

Included among the participants in Operation Delaware was the 26th Marine Regiment. The main goal of the Marines headed into A Shau was to draw contact from North Vietnamese units lurking in the valley. If the NVA could be drawn out of hiding, thereby giving away their positions, the American big guns—planes and heavy artillery—could be deployed to destroy the NVA staging areas. In essence, the Marine infantry units were being used as bait.

April 22, 1968

Dear Mom,

Well, as I assumed would eventually happen, beach duty ended yesterday, and my unit was put back into regular service. We have spent the last two days in a place called A Shau Valley. We were first introduced to A Shau yesterday morning when choppers flew the platoon to a landing zone deep in the heart of the valley. We then spent the entire day on reconnaissance missions in the jungle, looking for NVA.

A Shau Valley is nicknamed "Happy Valley," just like Penn State, but there is nothing remotely happy about it. In fact, going from Khe Sanh to A Shau may be like going from bad to worse.

In the two short days we have spent patrolling, we have already lost two members of our platoon, and two others were seriously wounded and needed to be medevaced out by helicopter. Aside from the persistent worry about ambushes, A Shau is loaded with booby traps. I'll be honest—it's scary there. It really works on a guy's nerves, knowing someone might jump out from a well-camouflaged hiding place and start shooting, or that you could just be walking along and end up setting off a land mine.

Fortunately, unlike at Khe Sanh, the combat in the valley is not nearly around the clock. At the end of the day, when the patrols are over, we return to Wonder Beach, which we use as a staging area, being shuttled back and forth to the valley by choppers. We are dropped off somewhere in the jungle, do our thing, and are picked up and returned to base. Sometimes, like today, we're even back in time for dinner. Speaking of which, I just noticed that it's time for chow. I'll write again soon.

Love,
Daniel

April 23, 1968

It was nearing 0900 when the Marine convoy slowed down on its approach to the military checkpoint located at the foot of the bridge. The guard manning the checkpoint stepped out from behind a barricade of sandbags, metal plates, and mounted machine guns, and directed the trucks to one side of the bridge. As the trucks came to a stop, the Marine platoon riding in the rear-holds filed off the vehicles and assembled along the edge of the road. To his delight, Dan's platoon would not be going into A Shau today. Instead, it had pulled bridge duty.

Bridge duty occurred at a series of three bridges adjacent to Route 1 that spanned the Rao Quan River. Each bridge housed military checkpoints, where Vietnamese civilians were checked for identification to make as certain as possible they were not NVA or Viet Cong. It was the responsibility of the Marines to monitor these checkpoints, and for today, that job fell to Dan's platoon.

In the afternoon of his first day of bridge duty, Dan found himself lounging atop a bunker located in a corner of the bridge to which his unit was assigned. So far, it had been an uneventful assignment. The area was considered secure, nothing at all like Khe Sanh or A Shau. No one worried about being shot or stepping on a land mine, and the greatest danger the Marines faced was severe sunburn. The view from Dan's vantage point was picturesque, marked by large trees covered with giant green leaves, and by a scenic panorama of the river and distant mountains. This particular bridge, which stretched several hundred feet across the river, had been designed with three thoroughfares, including a one-lane road for use by vehicles and bikes, a set of railroad tracks, and a plank pedestrian walkway that straddled the road. In each of the bridge's four corners sat a heavily fortified bunker. All four of those bunkers were mounted with an M-60. A fifth bunker, the command post, was situated in the middle of the bridge.

From his post, Dan relaxed and casually watched as US Navy gunboats patrolled the river, and locals from a nearby village fished the water. Sitting there, Dan secretly hoped the day would last forever, or at least until his tour was finished. The solitude of the moment was broken when Pappas climbed onto the roof of the bunker.

"What's up, Ralphie?" Dan asked.

"You're relieved, bro. It's my turn to man the sixty."

"I won't argue with you on that one," Dan said as he lowered himself off the roof and strolled leisurely from the bridge down to the bank of the river.

Arriving at the edge of the water, he took a seat next to Steve, Rodriguez, and Webb, who were lolling about on the softly packed dirt along the shoreline, and pulled out a cigarette.

"Man," Webb remarked after a few moments of silence, "this is the good life. Look how beautiful this is. And I don't worry about being killed here. I wish all of Vietnam could be like this. If it were, I might actually like this war."

The others silently nodded in agreement. Dan found it almost therapeutic to watch the local Vietnamese men and women fish, as they cast their nets into the water and scooped their catches into large reed baskets that they carried on their backs. The scene prompted him to reminisce about Philadelphia and fishing for trout with his friend Mike in Valley Green. It was a memory of better times.

That night, Dan resumed sitting bunker watch, manning one of the M-60s. Feeling drowsy from an afternoon in the sun, and struggling to stay awake, he began to nod off. Suddenly, out of the corner of his eye, he detected a figure walking very slowly on the road leading to the bridge. Immediately, his senses snapped to attention and his body froze in place.

Watching the silhouette, Dan's thoughts were consumed by the fear that if this was an enemy sapper, he was as good as dead. This dread of impending doom was magnified because Dan, knowing he would be manning the M-60, foolishly did not think to bring either his M-16 or his .45 with him. Even though the mounted M-60 was itself a serious weapon, it was facing the river, which was located in the opposite direction from where the shadowy figure was approaching. While it was possible to lift the M-60 off its mount, Dan knew he could not rotate the heavy gun without alerting the presumed enemy soldier to his presence. And he certainly could not move it quickly enough before the sapper, realizing Dan was there, opened fire. Given the circumstances, Dan concluded that the only weapons he could employ were his fists and helmet, so it followed that his most logical course of action was to crouch down and wait silent and motionless, hoping whoever was heading toward the bridge had not yet noticed him.

Dan watched as the figure reached the foot of the bridge, and then held his breath as the sound of clumsy footsteps resonated from the wood planks, giving away the intruder's position. When the footsteps were within a few feet of where Dan was situated, he sprung out of his hiding spot and over the top of the bunker, violently pouncing on the mystery figure. He started flailing away, punching with his fists and slamming his helmet, trying to wrestle away the intruder's rifle.

Hearing all the commotion, several Marines came rushing out of the bunker and broke up the fight. With the situation calmed and flashlights turned on, Dan realized that he had not attacked an NVA soldier, but rather Jack Barry, a new addition to the platoon. Under questioning from one of the sergeants, Barry promptly explained that he had simply gotten bored of sitting in his bunker, and had decided to take a walk. Needless to say, he was less than happy with Dan as he tended to a bloody nose. Dan, however, was hardly sympathetic. He reasoned Jack should have been smarter than to wander around in the middle of the night like that, and that on any other night, he would probably have gotten himself shot.

April 24, 1968
Journal Entry

Today was a bad day for us. For starters, we spent most of our morning patrolling A Shau in the midst of a driving downpour. Within the first half-hour of our patrol, the rain had seeped through our ponchos, saturating our uniforms, and our boots quickly became waterlogged. After five hours of relentless rain, it felt like the water had soaked right into our bones.

But the rain was a minor nuisance compared to the bloodshed we endured during the day's journey into the valley. Even though we spent no more than five hours sweeping through A Shau, we lost one Marine, and several others were severely wounded.

Turk was the first guy to get hit. He went down less than five minutes after we were off the chopper when he stepped on a land mine that blew off his right leg, just below the knee. He was covered in blood and in such pain that he kept repeating the same piercing scream, no matter what we did to try and keep him quiet. We certainly couldn't leave him there, but we were unable to carry him with us, either, so we had to radio the chopper that had just dropped us off to circle back and pick him up. Maybe an hour later, we found ourselves under attack when we drew sniper fire from a distant tree line. Fortunately, the sniper was not a very good shot, and he only managed to graze one of our guys before being silenced by our return fire.

The most depressing part of the whole operation, however, occurred toward the end, as we made our way back to the landing zone. Just fifteen short minutes from our rendezvous point with the choppers, our column walked smack into an NVA ambush. I remember one second I was complaining to myself about the constant rain and how tired I was of being on my feet, and then the next second, our point man, Buchholz, was shot dead. I watched as he crumpled to the ground, a split second before the crack of the shot even registered. Ryan and Adams were trailing closely behind. Several grenades landed right on top of them, and they both went down in a cloud of dirt and shrapnel. As the ambush unfolded, everyone not already hit dove for cover, letting loose heavy fire on the brush line from where the enemy was targeting us. I held down the trigger on my M-16 until it was empty, quickly reloaded, and resumed shooting. We continued exchanging gunfire for about a minute as the explosions echoed through the jungle. The fighting then ended as abruptly as it had started, and with equally little notice.

The deafening volley of gunfire was soon replaced by the spine-tingling screams of pain coming from Ryan and Adams. I looked around and saw three of my buddies on the ground, and expressions of shock on the faces of those who were not injured. As the doc pronounced Buchholz dead and began tending to the wounded, I turned away, tuning out the sounds of fear and anguish coming from the injured Marines. Having seen and heard the same scene all too often, I instead stared blankly into the jungle and listened to the patter of the incessant rain plopping on the leaves.

April 26, 1968
Dear Mom,
. . . After the horrible day we had in the valley, I guess someone decided we deserved some light duty. For the last two days, the platoon has been running security for a compound of Army engineers at an Esso refinery just north of Da Nang. While this assignment involves the usual gambit of day patrols, night ambushes, and LPs, the area around the Esso facility is considered much safer than A Shau. In fact, the biggest danger we have faced so far was posed by our own side.

Last night our squad was sent out on an ambush, and although command was tracking our exact movements the entire evening, somehow our communications still got all screwed up. As we hiked back onto the base from an otherwise uneventful evening in the field, a contingent of Army tanks mistook our unit for NVA and began shooting at us. Thank goodness a tank round has a flat trajectory, so we just laid low in a trench line as the tanks fired right over us. Still, the violently loud cracks of the tank shells, as well as the .50 caliber machine gun fire and accompanying tracer rounds, were enough to scare the heck out of all of us.

The tanks finally ceased firing, but only after some tense minutes of us cursing and hollering bloody hell over the radio to get them to stop. Luckily, no one was hurt, and today the Army issued an apology for the incident, but it didn't mean very much to any of us. With all the crap we have to deal with from the NVA, we don't have a lot of patience when it comes to our Army shooting at us. . . .

Love,
Daniel

April 27, 1968
Journal Entry

One of the hazards we face in A Shau that makes it so dangerous is all the booby traps the NVA have rigged throughout the valley. However, these aren't the swinging gates or elaborate punji pits like you see in the movies. Instead, most everything that we encounter is in the form of very rudimentary bombs constructed with grenades or land mines. These weapons are so simply constructed that young children could build them if you gave them the materials.

The device the NVA seems particularly fond of is a basic trip wire. This is fashioned by taking a grenade and tying it to a tree positioned off to the side of a trail they expect us to use. They then tie a wire to the pin of the grenade and string the wire, a few inches above the ground, across the path to a second tree. Someone will walk by and trip the wire, pulling the pin, and boom—some poor guy doesn't have a leg anymore.

We see stuff like that every time we go into the valley. While sitting on the chopper this morning, I gazed around at my friends, one by one. There were fifteen of us, and I began to wonder how many would still be around tomorrow. We all anticipate that something is going to happen to somebody whenever we head out on a mission. It is just a question of whom. I even caught myself looking at different guys and questioning which one we would lose next.

Considering that I'm not the only person having these thoughts, I can't say I'm surprised to hear that some fellows are beginning to get really messed up in the head. Honestly, I'm amazed that so many have held it together for this long. I mean, all this shit starts fucking with your mind pretty badly after a while. For example, I've heard guys discussing how it would be bad to lose a leg, but even worse to lose a hand. Then they rationalize that if they lose a hand, at least they'll still be alive and get to go home, so the loss of a hand wouldn't be so bad after all. It is these kinds of thoughts that can really play on one's nerves, and drive someone to near insanity.

April 28, 1968
Journal Entry

Last night marked our first overnight stay in A Shau, and before we even set up our positions, we sensed it was going to be a bad experience. Shortly before dusk, our patrol stopped at a point with thick ground cover several miles south of our landing zone. We hastily dug fighting positions into the muddy ground, setting up our holes so that they formed a perimeter in the shape of a circle. We took shelter from the persistent rain by sitting under our ponchos, which we propped up on sticks to form makeshift roofs. It has been pouring rain for three straight days now, and we are all pretty sick of it. We ate our C-rats while we sat in our cramped surroundings, whispering jokes to each other to keep from going stir-crazy. I thought for a moment about writing a letter home, but then decided against it. I'm writing with less frequency now, as I'm having more and more trouble keeping my emotions in check, and I'm concerned that I will worry my mother more than I already have.

As the hours passed, we desperately craved cigarettes to help calm our nerves, but refrained from smoking because we were warned that the light and smoke could give away our positions. Not that it ended up mattering anyway, as we probably could have smoked to our hearts' content and still not had a worse night. At around 2300, Charlie came at us, and came at us hard. They attacked in a concentrated formation, initially training their attack on one small section of the perimeter. When they were unsuccessful in breaching the perimeter on the first try, they backed off and attacked another area, trying to find a weak spot that they could penetrate. Fortunately, we stood our ground, and they withdrew.

When the firing finally stopped, and we began to assess the damage, we discovered our unit had suffered heavy casualties. Some of the wounded needed more medical attention than we could administer in the field, so a chopper was called in to evacuate them. When it landed, Walker, one of the new guys in our platoon, took advantage of the thick darkness and the distraction provided by the helicopter and climbed into the chopper, even though he was not wounded. It wasn't until this morning, when we counted heads and he was nowhere to be found, that we realized he was missing. This evening, after we got back to base, we made it a point to track down the helicopter pilot to see if he could provide us with any information. He remembered seeing that asshole on board, but assumed he was injured. When the chopper landed, Walker did a disappearing act, and now no one has any idea where he is, though there's a rumor that he's in some opium den in Saigon. Regardless of where they find him, he better be dead, because there are a couple of guys around here who would like to kill him if he isn't.

Anyway, this morning, after we took a count of personnel and determined what we had left to work with, we boarded choppers and flew up to the Esso facility. A group of Marine Corps engineers was heading out to make repairs to a bridge, and we were assigned to accompany the engineers' tank convoy and handle security. The ride sucked because we were simply seated on top of the tanks wherever we could find something to hold onto, while the engineers were tucked snuggly inside the tanks behind steel armor almost a foot thick. Such is the life of an expendable grunt.

As the tanks were rumbling through the countryside, bouncing and jarring us all over the metal plating, not surprisingly we started to draw sniper fire from a distant tree line. Immediately, the tanks came skidding to a halt so the gunners could return fire, and all of us perched on top went flying onto the muddy road. As we picked our bruised bodies off the ground, the tanks' turrets rotated and let loose on the tree line, putting an end to the sniper fire.

Although none of the sniper fire connected, Zack, one of the Marines who happened to be riding with me, ended up breaking his arm when he was tossed off the tank and slammed to the ground. I could tell something was wrong the second Zack hit the road surface with a loud thud, because he began cursing in pain. At first, he was so pissed off that we had to hold him back from getting into a fistfight with the tank operator. However, as soon as the doc examined him and told him his arm was broken, Zack became overwhelmed with joy, expecting that his injury would probably get him discharged. He was soon dancing around and hugging everybody in sight, including the tank driver, who just moments earlier he had wanted to deck.

April 29, 1968
Journal Entry

After a long couple of days in the field, we intended to spend our evening in the barracks here at the Esso plant, listening to the rain patter against the tin roof. We had received orders to conduct a night ambush not far outside the base perimeter, but we were totally exhausted from the previous days' activities. Our decision to hang out was also influenced by the fact that we were experiencing our fourth straight day of steady rain. We just plain needed a break from war. As we lounged in the warm, dry confines of our barracks, playing cards and writing letters, a lieutenant from another platoon paid us a chance visit and caught us skipping out on our patrol.

When he discovered that we were playing hooky from work, he began cursing and screaming, rambling on about how we were supposed to be out on ambush, that we were disobeying orders, and so on. The lieutenant then ordered us to grab our gear and leave the barracks. Once we were all outside, he had us line up against the wall of the building, where he continued his curse-filled tirade, calling us pussies and cowards, and ranting about how we should all receive court-martials. Being that we cared little about what he had to say, we stood there impatiently, hoping he would tire of berating us so we could get out of the rain and go back to playing cards. What he did next, though, was completely unexpected. Apparently frustrated that we were unresponsive to his threats, the son of a bitch brazenly pulled out his .45, chambered a round, and started waving the gun in our faces.

While true that he was a lieutenant, and we were mostly all just privates and corporals, many of us were also Khe Sanh vets. We did not take kindly to being intimidated by some officer from another unit sticking a loaded gun in our faces. No way were we going to let him try to pull rank on us and threaten us with bodily harm. To emphasize that we were not about to put up with his shit, we all started to let the bolts on our M-16s slide home and slowly leveled our muzzles. Once he realized we weren't playing around and he was very much outgunned, he stopped screaming, holstered his gun, and calmly walked away without saying another word.

April 30, 1968
Journal Entry

There's this little joke we have, about how when we fly into A Shau we do so with big targets painted on our backs. The joke stems from the perception that whenever we go into the valley we're sitting ducks, mainly because the NVA has a complete lock on the element of surprise. They always know when we're coming into the valley just by listening and watching for our helicopters. Once we're on the ground, it's very easy for them to monitor our movements without being detected, this being the result of the jungle providing them with so much cover. On the flip side, usually the only time we know their location is when they're shooting at us.

This morning was a perfect example of how they flat-out control the element of surprise. As we landed our choppers, they were waiting to ambush us at the landing zone. The first guy getting off my chopper, Barbarisi, got shot right in his balls the moment he stepped onto the pad. I swear, I've never seen anyone in my life in more pain. It was so horrible, I don't even want to get into the details. A split-second later, Corrigan, who was the next guy off the chopper, got shot in his arm, the bullet shattering his bones.

Realizing we were being ambushed, the M-60 gunner began laying cover fire, and the few of us who had a clear line of sight from the chopper cabin began firing into the tree line. Barbarisi and Corrigan, who were both lying on the ground near the foot of the landing skid, were hastily pulled back onto the chopper, and we became airborne again. The whole scene was crazy, but the rough part about it was that we never stood a chance. The NVA had our number as soon as we took off from the base to fly into the valley.

May 1, 1968

Dan stood at the center of the bridge, smoking a cigarette and watching the Vietnamese locals fishing in the river below. After an early morning rain, the day had turned beautiful, and from his vantage point the water looked gorgeous against the backdrop of a clear blue sky. The air was crisp yet tropical, but not overbearingly humid as it could so frequently be in Vietnam. Dan remained caught up in his own world, admiring the view, when Steve ambled over.

"What's going on, Dan?" he asked.

"Not much, man. I'm just relaxing, watching the locals fish."

Joining Dan, Steve comfortably leaned himself against the thin railing that protected passers-by from falling several stories into the water below. The two friends silently observed the locals working the riverbanks with nets, tree lines, and rudimentary homemade fishing poles, plying a trade they had been honing for generations.

"Man, these villagers are going about this fishing thing all wrong," Steve said, breaking the silence. "That's no way to fish. I bet you a pack of cigarettes I could catch twice as many fish as any of these locals."

"What the hell are you talking about?" Dan asked, puzzled by Steve's seemingly silly remarks. Having witnessed firsthand the scores of men, women, and children effortlessly haul in a multitude of fish while he had stood on the bridge, Dan doubted that the locals required any help or advice. They certainly did not need any suggestions from Steve. "They look like they know exactly what they're doing. I wish I had half as much luck fishing back home in the Wissahickon Creek."

"Well, like I said," Steve replied, as a broad, knowing smile spread across his face, "that's not how you fish."

Then, in one quick, continuous motion, and before Dan even had time to react, Steve yanked a grenade off his flak jacket, pulled its pin, and hurled it high into the air. He threw it far from the bridge, much closer to where the locals were fishing than to where the two Marines now stood. Dan tracked the grenade's flight as it dropped into the river, and could only stare at the grenade's point of entry into the water, and then at the ripples it stirred as the tiny waves spread toward the shore. Dan was so stunned and shocked by what Steve had just done that he found himself unable to even smile at the absurdity of his friend's conduct.

Seconds later, the grenade exploded, and a plume of water emerged high into the air. The villagers congregating along the river's edge, believing that the Marines guarding the bridge were under attack, went scampering for cover. But when no additional explosions materialized, they gradually emerged from their hiding places and returned to the riverbank. As they reappeared, they were greeted by dozens of dead fish floating on the surface of the river. Quickly forgetting their fears from a moment ago, the villagers scurried into the water to collect the bountiful gift Steve had just provided. They waded in up to their waists and scooped up every fish floating on the water's surface, carrying them off in reed baskets, nets, and even the shirts they were wearing.

Watching this comical series of events unfold, and no longer horrified at the thought of the potentially disastrous outcomes of Steve's actions, Dan let out a burst of unconstrained laughter.

Steve turned to Dan, his chest bulging with pride and a huge smile crossing his face, and proudly exclaimed, "Now that's the way to fish!"

—

That evening, several of the Marines in Dan's platoon proceeded to consume a case of beer they had appropriated from an officer of another unit. One of the guys drinking was known to have a real problem holding his liquor, and when intoxicated, he turned violent and uncontrollable. Sure enough, his behavior on this night would be no different. Severely drunk and barely able to stay upright, he became hell-bent on going to the local village, located just a few hundred yards from the bridge, and getting laid in their whorehouse. Some of his buddies tried to talk him out of it, but those discussions ended the moment he pulled out his combat knife and dared anyone to try and stop him.

About an hour later, as Dan and several other Marines lay on the beach along the river listening to water splash up against the shore, the quiet peace of the night was disrupted by a series of screams followed by gunfire coming from the direction of the village. The platoon members grabbed their weapons and moved toward the village, worried it might be under attack by the NVA. However, upon entering the village, the Marines were met by several locals who pointed them not to some strategic location on an overlooking hill, but to the whorehouse. On inspection, the platoon came upon the drunken Marine passed out on the floor of the brothel's entrance. Next to him lay his M-16 and an empty ammunition clip. Fortunately, he had not shot anyone, but the whorehouse was ransacked. For his indiscretion, and in an apparent attempt to save face with the villagers, he was escorted away by military police once he was revived.

May 2, 1968
Journal Entry

I dread going into A Shau Valley. Each trip is its own ordeal, almost as agonizing as the hell we suffered at Khe Sanh. The countless booby traps and recurring NVA ambushes are really beginning to take their toll on the unit. We frequently stumble across trip wires connected to hand grenades, or other simply constructed explosive devices designed to maim as much as they are to kill. It's to the point where I'm afraid to move because I'm worried I'll step on a land mine or blow myself up some other way. It seems like every time we go into A Shau we are fired upon or come across booby traps, and more Marines die.

Less apparent than the physical losses we are suffering is the mental toll that these incidents are inflicting. When the shooting starts, everything we've ever been taught goes out the window. As well trained as we are, we're still human beings, and it's all too easy to become frightened, consumed, and overwhelmed by the fear and confusion. At times, I'm such an emotional mess after things go down, or after someone is killed, that I just sit and shake uncontrollably. I never tell anyone how scared I am, though, because I'm a Marine. A Marine is trained to be squared-away, tough, and not afraid of anything or anyone. Marines aren't supposed to be scared. Marines are expected to be bad asses. But that's not reality. When the tracers fly overhead, or the unmistakable sound of a fired bullet cracks in your ear, terror can overwhelm even the toughest of Marines.

When the shit does hit the fan, often the only thing that keeps me from freezing up and being unable to react is a sudden burst of adrenaline pumping through my body. In those instances when I am overcome by fear, my heart will feel like it's beating 1,000 times a minute, and I'll feel nauseous, like I want to vomit. But I believe this fear also helps keep me alive, because it sparks a sense of awareness of my surroundings.

I know other guys get scared, too, even if it's not a subject they openly discuss. If they aren't shaking, vomiting, or crying, you can still see the fear in their eyes. They have this unmistakable look on their faces, as if they're afraid to die and know they just came really close to getting it. No one wants to even consider the possibility of dying, but we are all too aware that at any moment it could be our turn. I worry plenty about it, too. I would be lying if I claimed I don't think about my life coming to an end. Every time someone is killed, I tell myself that I have to get out of here. I become nervous whenever it occurs to me that as long as I remain in this place, sooner or later it's going to be my turn to be the one who is dead.

May 3, 1968

Dear Mom,

How are you? I hope that you are not spending too much of your days worrying about me. I'm sure whatever you are hearing about on the news is being exaggerated. We'll be fine as long as we can stay out of our own way. Yesterday, for example, our platoon was running security at the Esso plant when, in the early evening, we received word over the radio that the platoon on bridge duty was engaged in heavy fighting and needed help. By the time we reached the bridge, the NVA had retreated into the nearby village, which we were ordered to encircle. With reinforcements arriving from several other platoons, Marines were placed as little as ten feet from one another around the village's border in order to prevent any of the NVA from escaping. Meanwhile, Navy gunboats were called in to patrol the river along the village shore. We had the enemy surrounded. The plan, as it was explained, was to keep them trapped in the area until daylight, when we would storm the village.

During the middle of the night, the same lieutenant, who I think in one of my letters I told you had tried to get in our faces with his .45, came walking down our line. He wasn't taking any precautions to stay low to the ground or talk in a hushed tone. Worried he would give away our positions and get us killed, some guys started mockingly telling the lieutenant that he needed to stay down and be quiet so that he wouldn't draw enemy fire. Not willing to take advice from grunts, he ignored our warnings, reminding us that he was a ranking officer and the one who gave the orders, and not the other way around.

Not interested in exposing our positions any more than they may already have been revealed, we stopped arguing with him, hoping he would continue down our line as quickly as possible. However, about thirty or forty yards from my point, he must have heard some rustling in a patch of brush, because he abruptly took a few steps toward it and started shining his flashlight into the shrubs. He then hollered something about the Marine in the brush needing to stop goofing off.

Still shining his flashlight, he proceeded to reach into the brush, and grabbing the person's uniform collar, pulled into the open what he thought was a Marine. But instead of a Marine, the lieutenant had grabbed hold of a North Vietnamese soldier trying to sneak out of the village. The NVA soldier quickly twisted out of the lieutenant's grasp and opened fire with his AK-47, somehow miraculously completely missing the lieutenant, who was standing only a few feet away. The lieutenant, terrified and probably peeing his pants, dropped to the ground. With the lieutenant out of the line of fire, several Marines let loose with their M-16s before the NVA soldier could flee, shooting him close to fifty times. After the firing stopped, the lieutenant meekly walked away, not even taking a second to look back at the body. We snickered for a couple of minutes after that one. Not surprisingly, the lieutenant didn't show his face around us following the incident.

Anyway, so that you aren't left wondering how the story ends, at dawn we moved into the village as planned, but did so without meeting any NVA resistance. It turns out that the NVA used the cover of darkness to escape through weak links in our lines. They snuck out right under our noses, and there was little we could do about it. It was just another typical night in Vietnam. Well, take care, and I'll write again soon.
Love,
Daniel

May 4, 1968
At the moment, Dan really wished he were anywhere else but Vietnam. His platoon lay motionless behind a thick camouflage of jungle cover, staring into the darkness. At dusk, they had received orders to go out on an ambush, and had trudged two miles in the dark to their current position, which overlooked a suspected North Vietnamese infiltration route.

Sitting in the dank, dirty, inhospitable jungle, Dan was experiencing severe physical discomfort due to having remained essentially motionless for the past two hours, and was having more difficulty than normal in keeping his nerves under control. Adding to the discomfort were the heat and humidity, along with his impression that he was being eaten alive by mosquitoes.

There was no moon this evening, and the gloomy jungle gave him the creeps. Every time he looked toward the kill zone, he spooked himself, thinking a tree stump or a rock was an NVA soldier moving in on his position. Worse still, Dan's stomach turned slightly each time he considered the prospect of what might happen if they were to encounter some NVA. He had long ago received his fill of bloodshed, and he could really do without more of it tonight. Unfortunately, tonight was not one from which to expect favors.

Another hour of tense waiting passed, when all at once the jungle moved. Dan froze in place, and he could sense that the whole platoon had stiffened in expectation of what was to come next. Everyone waited for the sergeant in command to open fire, as the orders were to shoot only after he did. Dan watched as the shadowy silhouette of a large NVA column passed barely yards in front of the Marines' U-shaped ambush. The enemy was so close that he could hear them talking. Focused on the sergeant out of the corner of his eye, Dan uneasily anticipated the imminent hell that would result from the actions of the dozen-and-a-half young Marines. Sweat was pouring down his face and stinging his eyes, but he didn't dare lift his arm to wipe it away. Instead, he held his breath, afraid to make the slightest noise or move even the most insignificant muscle. He was keenly aware of the loud thumping his heart made as it beat rapidly in his chest. He really fucking hated this.

The lead of the NVA column finally reached the far end of the kill zone where an M-60 gunner was positioned, and on cue, the sergeant opened fire. All of a sudden, the night was ablaze with the gunfire of M-16s and M-60s and the tremendous explosions of claymore mines and grenades. The dark jungle turned into the military equivalent of a disco dance floor, illuminated by a strobe light of gunfire and bombs. Seconds later, as a number of the platoon members hurried to change clips, the sergeant called out for everyone to cease firing. Dan loaded a new magazine into his weapon, and then cautiously stood up so that he could see the kill zone. Sickened by the sight of a kill zone littered with more bodies than he could ever recall seeing in one place at any single time, he turned away in revulsion.

The radio crackled.

"What happened, team leader? Are you all right? Repeat, are you all right?"

The staff sergeant picked up the receiver and pushed the button to reply.

"Roger that. We're all right. Charlie's caught in the web."

"What are the casualties, team leader?"

As the question came across the radio, Roland Dean was picking his way along the trail, counting the NVA bodies.

"My God," he called back to the sergeant in disbelief. "We must have killed hundreds of them."

Minutes later, Dean was wishing he had responded that the NVA had all managed to elude the trap. While the number of killed was closer to several dozen than hundreds, it was still an impressive tally as far as body counts went. The captain on the other end of the radio, hearing about the success of the ambush, and hoping for a large body count that he could document for his superiors, wanted to see the bodies for himself. However, inasmuch as he was not willing to hike two miles at night, through terrain swarming with enemy fighters, the platoon was ordered to drag over thirty bodies back through the jungle, just so the captain could personally verify his body count.

May 5, 1968
Dear Mom,

I thought I would write and tell you a funny anecdote, so that you don't assume that everything around here is all doom and gloom. Remember how I was telling you about bridge duty? Well, a key responsibility we have when we are serving on bridge duty is to protect it from amphibious assaults. One of the ways we go about doing this is that every thirty minutes or so, we lower sticks of dynamite, tied to long ropes, down from the walkway on the bridge to the bottom of the river. We then detonate the dynamite to discourage the NVA from swimming up to the bridge and wiring it with explosives.

Today we were on bridge duty, going through this routine of dynamiting the river. As we began lowering the ropes, a local passenger train approaching the bridge interrupted us. Trains in Vietnam are not like the modern, comfortable trains we have in the US. These trains are rickety old things that are always packed to the brim with far more passengers than there are seats. No matter the number of these trains we see, I'm always just amazed at how many people can actually be crowded onto them.

As this particular train approached, we couldn't help but notice that this one appeared even more packed than usual. Each passenger car was overflowing with ARVN soldiers. There were ARVN hanging off the sides, ARVN sitting on the roofs, and ARVN sticking out of the windows. The scene reminded me of those television contests where the goal is to cram as many people as possible into the confines of a phone booth or automobile.

Anyway, as the train started rolling onto the bridge, I heard my buddy Jay-Jay yelling to get my attention over the noise of the locomotive. I turned toward him and watched as he began to lower a stick of dynamite into the river. However, instead of dropping the dynamite to the bottom of the river, he placed it only about three or four feet under the surface of the water. I immediately knew exactly what he was up to—he was going to try to soak the train. He tied off the rope, and the two of us ran to the end of the bridge. We waited until the train was directly over the dynamite, and then Jay-Jay hit the detonator. A split second later, there was a huge explosion, and water flew into the air over the train and then cascaded down onto the bridge in a thick sheet. For a few seconds, the water engulfed the train's cars, and the ARVN soldiers hanging off the cars were completely soaked.

Jay-Jay fell to the ground in hysterical laughter. However, my laughter was tempered by sudden fear, brought about by what I had noticed immediately prior to the detonation of the dynamite. In the moment before the trigger was hit, I spotted a lieutenant crossing the rickety plank walkway that spanned the bridge. When the water flew up from the river, he disappeared behind the wall of water. Meanwhile, the walkway planks, which were not secured very well, went flying away in the torrent of water.

To my relief, when the water fell back into the river, the soaking wet lieutenant was standing on the last remaining walkway plank near where the explosion had been triggered. The slats in front of and behind him were missing, and only his own body weight had kept the plank on which he was standing from being blown away. Relieved that the lieutenant was not dead or hurt, I joined in Jay-Jay's laughter. What I found most amusing was the irony of two members of the greatest and most sophisticated fighting force in the world being able to ambush one of their own lieutenants, as well as an entire ARVN company, using nothing more than a stick of dynamite and a river. . . .

Love,
Daniel

♠

Chapter 13

-May 6-

*"Circles round my head
of friends dear friends
who talk to me
of happy times
past present and the future."*

-Leslie Levinson

Dan clumsily ran toward the choppers as his equipment bounced awkwardly against his body. His gear was extra heavy this morning because the platoon was given orders to pack a double load of ammunition, adding many pounds to the weight of his bag. Reaching the foot of a chopper, he climbed onto the deck, ducked underneath the idling blades, and plopped down next to Steve and Rodriguez. It was still early in the morning, around 0500, and Dan's stomach, filled with scrambled eggs and coffee from the breakfast he had just gobbled down, was a bit queasy in anticipation of today's mission. With the last Marine on board, the pilots pulled off the landing zone. The cool, misty air of the morning blew across the open deck of the helicopter, sending chills down Dan's back. He sat silently as the hum of the blades, combined with the noise from the wind whipping through the deck, overwhelmed any attempts at conversation.

The platoon had received orders to fly into A Shau and conduct a sweep through a portion of the valley that had recently become a hotbed of violent encounters with NVA forces. The morning's area of operation also contained a South Vietnamese village that the military believed was serving as a cover for one of the NVA staging areas in the region. Entering the village would be their day's primary objective. As the entire sector was heavily infested with NVA forces, the Marines knew that if enemy fighters engaged them, the fighting could become intense. Unnerved by the potential ugliness of today's hostilities, Dan spent his time in the air looking out onto the jungles of Vietnam, and calmed himself as best he could by thinking about Robbie and family and friends back in Philadelphia.

Eventually, the choppers carrying the platoon reached the ridgeline that marked the border of A Shau. As they flew over the ridge, heading into the heart of the valley, Dan could make out large patches of scorched jungle destroyed by bombing raids and napalm strikes. It was a sight to which he had become accustomed, and one that most poignantly symbolized the devastation the war had inflicted on what was once a strikingly beautiful country. The helicopters continued to push farther and deeper into A Shau, finally touching down on a makeshift landing zone. As they taxied, the Marines jumped off the decks and scampered twenty yards into tall grass, which blew wildly in the wind being kicked up by the whirling helicopter blades. Crouching low, in case there were any NVA lying in wait for them, Dan clicked off the safety on his M-16 and scanned the tree line fifty yards in front of him. As soon as their decks were clear, the choppers took back to the air, leaving the platoon to the valley. The Marines formed on-line and headed toward the trees.

As the platoon entered the jungle through the tree line, the pace of the troops slowed and became more deliberate, everyone vividly aware of the dangers A Shau presented. An eerie feeling came over Dan as the bare skin on his arms brushed against the damp dew still clinging to the overgrown foliage. To the platoon's rear, the sun tried to make its way over the rising hills that surrounded the area.

After an hour of trudging through thick overgrowth, the Marines found themselves cautiously advancing toward an opening in the dense jungle, and halted their march roughly ten yards before the cover of the trees gave way to a grass clearing. The platoon was ordered down on their bellies, and the Marines used the opportunity to drink water and double-check their equipment. The sergeant leading the patrol got onto the radio, surveying his map while he communicated with headquarters. From where he lay, Dan observed another tree line roughly fifty yards on the other side of the clearing in front of them. He could also faintly make out the target village, which was located just beyond the second tree line. Dan peered ahead anxiously, contemplating what might lie hidden among the trees on the far side of the field, in the direction of which they no doubt would soon be ordered to advance. Five minutes later, the platoon was back on its feet, moving out into the open expanse, no longer in single file, but in a formation that spread the Marines so that they were positioned parallel to both tree lines.

As Dan emerged from the trees, he surveyed the unbroken field of grass in front of him with great apprehension. He nervously pressed forward, keenly aware of the waist high grass gently swaying against his body in the light breeze. Reaching the middle of the field, Dan quickened his step but restrained himself from getting too far out in front. He dreaded being in the open where he was fully exposed, and the fifty yards to the other side of the clearing seemed a mile away.

Suddenly, Dan's worst fears were realized. Without warning, the tree line toward which the Marines were heading erupted with gunfire. Before ever having the chance to take cover, he was thrown face first onto the ground by a loud explosion only yards away. The concussion knocked him into a daze, as if he had just been smacked square in the face with a punch from a heavyweight prizefighter. As he lay there, trying to clear his head, Dan attempted to roll over onto his back, but found that he could not move. Although he felt no pain, his body still in shock and numb from the explosion, Dan knew something was terribly wrong.

"It can't be that bad," he thought to himself.

Again, he tried to turn over, but was unable to do so. Never before in his life was Dan ever this petrified with fear.

He somehow finally gathered enough strength in his arms to roll himself onto his back. At that moment, he became absorbed with his own condition, oblivious to the rest of the world and the fighting and explosions around him. He could not hear the deafening gunfire coming from both his unit and from the NVA who were shooting at the Marines from the tree line. He could not hear the shouts and screams of the other Marines, some writhing in agony from wounds, others trying to impose some semblance of organization on the scattered platoon. He did not see the tracers darting from seemingly every direction, or the thin haze of gun smoke rapidly forming in the air. Dan did not flinch, as he normally would have, when another explosive round landed close enough to where he was lying to send dirt flying into his face. Everything seemed to be moving in slow motion, the world around him silent but for the sound of his own thoughts.

With great difficulty, Dan hesitantly lifted his head and looked down the length of his body. His flak jacket was torn apart and his pants ripped to shreds. There was blood everywhere, and what remained of his uniform was slowly becoming soaked dark red. Mixed in with the blood, he could see black residue from the gunpowder of the explosive charge that had knocked him down. Smoke from the heat generated by the explosion was coming off his body, like the morning mist rising off a lake. The whole scene seemed surreal.

Then, all at once, after a period of time that felt like minutes, but in actuality lasted just seconds, Dan snapped back into reality. As if a switch was flipped, the pain rushed into his body, and he began to scream. He didn't cry out for anyone or for anything in particular—he just screamed. With each passing second, his shrill, frightened screams became louder and louder. Dan was terrified. He was now aware of the gunfire and explosions occurring all around him, and this unnerved him even further. It didn't take more than a few moments before his shrieks caught the attention of the NVA. Immediately, the ground kicked up around him, and then several bullets pierced his body. He experienced excruciating pain, like sharp, hot nails being driven through his flesh.

Then, unexpectedly, Dan felt a hand. It was Rodriguez's hand, and it was grabbing Dan's arm. Rodriguez gripped Dan tightly and started dragging him backwards toward the tree line from where they had advanced moments earlier. Simultaneously, Rodriguez attempted to provide them both with covering fire from his M-16.

Dan was rapidly losing blood, and only vaguely aware of what was happening. He could feel the ground moving beneath him as stones and branches dug into his back, but had no idea of his location or to where he was being pulled. Seconds later, his head bounced against the jungle floor and he lost consciousness.

When he awoke, Dan could see out of the corners of his eyes that other bodies had been placed next to him. He could faintly make out machine gun fire that, although it seemed a mile away, was actually occurring in close proximity to where he was lying. Dan closed his eyes and heard the humming sound of helicopters in the distance. A gust of wind whipped the tree branches and blew leaves and debris across his face. He felt dizzy and light-headed, his body in excruciating agony. His clothes were warm and sticky as blood matted the fabric against his body. Even though his flesh burned with searing pain where he had been wounded, chills crept up his neck, and he began to feel cold flashes. A moment later, Dan again blacked out.

The next thing Dan saw was the blurry figure of the helicopter crew chief standing over him. It appeared to Dan as if the crew chief was trying to scream something in his ear, but he could not be sure because he could hear no sounds. Within another minute or so, he again lost awareness of what was happening around him.

When he regained consciousness, Dan found himself being lifted onto an operating table. Looking around to determine his whereabouts, he observed doctors and nurses scrambling every which way, while others were ripping off his clothing and inserting tubes into his arms and chest. Before passing out for the final time that day, Dan strained to focus through the sea of green surgical uniforms worn by those around him. Looking up, he made eye contact with the man now standing directly over him holding a scalpel in his hand. Realizing he was about to go into surgery, Dan summoned a final gasp of strength and spoke.

"Doc," he whispered, "don't let me die."

Chapter 14

-The Journey Home-

"Take a shower, shine your shoes
you got no time to lose
you are young men you must be living
go now you are forgiven."

-Dispatch, *"General"*

```
P GVA014 XV GOVT PD WASHINGTON DC MAY 8 951A EDT
  MRS CHRISTINE M SULLIVAN
  222 NORTH MASCHER ST PHILA
THIS IS TO CONFIRM THAT YOUR SON PRIVATE FIRST CLASS DANIEL
J SULLIVAN USMC WAS INJURED 6 MAY 1968 IN THE VICINITY OF
QUANG TRI, REPUBLIC OF VIETNAM . HE SUSTAINED MULTIPLE
FRAGMENTATION WOUNDS TO BOTH LEGS BOTH ARMS HEAD AND TO THE LEFT SIDE
FROM A HOSTILE EXPLOSIVE DEVICE WHILE ON PATROL. HE IS
PRESENTLY RECEIVING TEREATMENT AT THE STATION HOSPITAL DANANG.
HIS CONDITION IS FAIR WITH HIS PROGNOSIS GOOD. YOUR ANXIETY IS
REALIZED AND YOU ARE ASSURED THAT HE IS RECEIVING THE VERY BEST
OF CARE. YOU WILL BE KEP INFORMED OF ALL SIGNIFICENT CHANGES IN
HIS CONDITION, HIS MAILING ADDRESS REMAINS THE SAME
    LEONARD J CHAPMAN JR GENERAL USMC COMMANDANT
OF THE MARINE CORPS
                1215PM
```

May 8, 1968

As he awoke for the first time since undergoing surgery, light began to filter into Dan's eyes. Blinking uncomfortably, he tried adjusting to light to which his eyes had not been exposed in almost two days. After a minute or so, his eyes began to clear. The first image he recognized was that of a young woman dressed in a starched white nurse's uniform hovering over him. Dan was confused. His head was encased in a drowsy fog, and he was having difficulty recollecting what had brought him to this situation. Looking down at his prone body, he observed that his arms were wrapped with bandages and the remainder of his body was dressed in light blue pajamas. Slowly, he surveyed his surroundings. His bed sat in a long, white corridor, and there were nurses and doctors everywhere. A row of beds ran along each side of the room, and a wounded soldier occupied almost every bed.

Then, as if struck by a bolt of lightning that jogged his memory, everything came rushing back to him. He remembered the firefight, the loud explosion, the gunfire, and being shot while he lay on the ground. Suddenly, a wave of nausea passed through him.

"Well, it is good to see you awake, Sullivan," the nurse said in a sweet, comforting voice, once she became aware that Dan was again conscious. "You should consider yourself lucky. You were wounded pretty seriously, but you should be all right. The doctors did a good job with you."

The nurse leaned over to check his bandages, and Dan noticed the way she smelled. She was not covered with perfume, yet the fragrance of her cleanliness, the scent of body soap and shampoo, stood in stark contrast to the rank odors he had experienced over the past months.

"Hey, nurse, what happened to me?" Dan asked weakly. "I mean, where was I hit?" The nurse reached over, picked up the clipboard hanging from the foot of the bed, and scanned it with glancing eyes.

"Says here you took grenade shrapnel in your arms, legs, and stomach, and that you were grazed in the head, and shot in the stomach, each leg, and in one foot. It looks like you were hit five times in all."

"Five times," Dan intoned in disbelief. And he was struck by a grenade, too. Indeed, he thought to himself, he was very lucky to be alive.

—

Later that day, a general, trailed by an entourage of lower-ranking officers and a team of military photographers, filed through the hospital ward. The general went from bed to bed, handing out Purple Hearts to the soldiers who had not yet received their medals. He would approach a bed, pin the purple, heart-shaped medal on the serviceman's chest, and perfunctorily shake the wounded soldier's hand while smiling for the cameras. Without wasting any time, the general would then robotically move to the next bed and again perform the same ritual for the cameras. As far as Dan was concerned, the whole process more resembled a factory assembly line than a series of reverent ceremonies.

Again and again, the general repeated the same exact bedside ceremony for nearly thirty soldiers, including Dan. When it all ended, and the procession left the room, Dan took a deep breath and almost choked from the thick stench of empty gratitude and less than heartfelt emotion displayed by the general and those accompanying him.

May 9, 1968

The injured soldiers fell quiet as the aluminum hospital bed was rolled into the hospital ward. Every wounded American serviceman watched in astonishment and disbelief as a team of nurses placed a wounded NVA soldier in the same room with them. No one said a single word, as an eerie silence enveloped the ward. Could this really be happening, they wondered? How could the nurses have such audacity and exhibit such insensitivity? Could they really be that ignorant? How many of the soldiers lying there at this moment were suffering from wounds inflicted by this North Vietnamese son of a bitch, or by one of his NVA or Viet Cong comrades?

After fifteen minutes of awkward stillness, the uneasy calm was broken when one of the American soldiers threw his urinal pan across the aisle that separated the two rows of beds, hitting the NVA soldier, and splashing him with urine. Taking their cue, other soldiers immediately grabbed whatever they could easily reach—urinal pans, clipboards, and food trays, and tossed them across the room, pelting the NVA soldier with the barrage. One of the nurses, a young American woman in her early twenties, came rushing into the ward, hollering for the soldiers to behave.

"Please, stop," she pleaded as she tried to shield the NVA soldier.

"Hey, lady," one of the wounded soldiers yelled back at her. "That fucking gook was out there killing us, and you want us to share space with the motherfucker?"

Enraged further by the message conveyed in his own words, the soldier grabbed the clipboard off his bed and hurled it like a Frisbee, so that it hit the wall right above where the Vietnamese soldier lay. The nurse, visibly shaken, stormed out of the room without another word. Less than a minute later, a team of nurses reentered the ward and quickly rolled the NVA soldier to another section of the hospital, never to be seen again.

May 11, 1968
Dear Mom,
I'm sorry I have not written you sooner, but I've just been too weak and tired to even lift a pencil. I am sure you have heard by now what happened to me. To put your fears to rest, I'm fine. In case you don't believe me, I have included some Polaroids taken by one of the orderlies to prove that I am all in one piece. I'm still very sore and awfully weak, but every single body part is intact. The docs say that I will probably have a limp for a while, and that there will be some scarring, but I don't really care. All that's important is that I'm alive and coming home.

Anyway, I spent the last few days confined to bed, but now I have healed enough to move around the hospital with the use of a wheelchair. My legs still hurt too much for me to walk on them, although the docs say they should be better eventually. My main problem, though, is that I haven't gotten my strength back yet. Just writing this letter has tired me out. I will try to write again when I have more energy. Talk to you soon.
Love,
Daniel

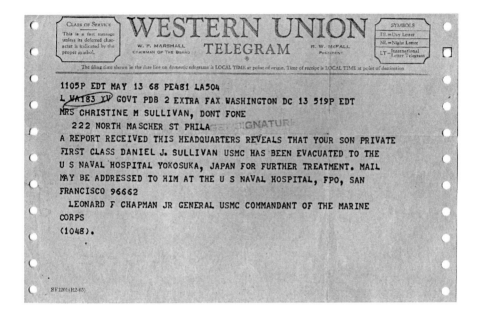

May 13, 1968
Journal Entry

As if the consequences of fighting in a war were not enough to deal with, at around 1800, Japan was hit with an earthquake. I was lying in bed when, unexpectedly, everything started shaking violently. Windows were shattered, lights flickered, and food trays and bedpans fell to the floor. Big, strong military types were reduced to yelling for help from nurses because they wanted to seek cover, but were unable to get themselves out of bed. The earthquake itself couldn't have lasted more than ten seconds, but it scared some guys pretty badly. How ironic to see a bunch of battle-hardened soldiers, witnesses to so much violence, many of whom had suffered near-death experiences in Vietnam, unnerved by a relatively minor earthquake.

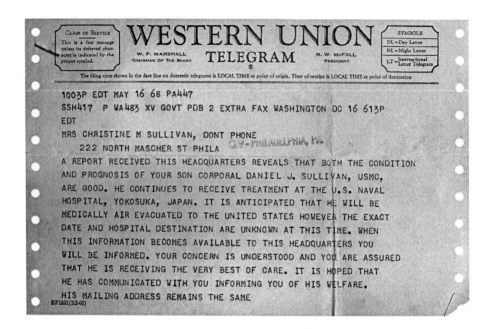

May 17, 1968

Dear Mom,

The docs tell me that I'm going to be here in Japan for at least a couple of months, but that's fine with me. I am overjoyed in the knowledge that I'm alive and will never again return to Vietnam to fight. It makes me proud that I didn't let those bastards kill me, just as I promised myself, even though I know my survival had a lot to do with luck.

When I'm not watching television or "The Good, the Bad, and the Ugly" for the millionth time, since it is the only movie they have here, I'm doing a lot of reminiscing. I often think about the guys in my unit that I left behind, and I worry about how they're getting along. I have tried to find out who else was injured on the 6th, or if anyone didn't make it, but things here are so disorganized that there's little information available. I try to get in touch with Rodriguez, but communicating with units in the field is impossible. I think about Robbie a great deal. Also, I speculate about whether everything on my body is going to work properly when I leave here. I'm told that I'll be able to start walking with crutches soon, but that I will also probably be walking with a limp for quite a while. However, that all sure sounds better to me than being dead. Mostly, though, I think about coming home. It won't be soon enough that I can get the hell out of this place. I'll see you then. I can't wait.

Love,
Daniel

May 20, 1968
Journal Entry

Being wounded, it turns out, is not the most unpleasant experience of my life. For example, I'm offered all the ice cream I can eat, and I'm allowed to watch television all day long. Then there are the sponge baths from the nurses. If I'd known about the sponge baths, I might have stepped in the way of an enemy bullet a long time ago. Also, although I'm stuck in a wheelchair for now, I enjoy racing through the hallways across the linoleum floors, and watching other guys engaging in wheelchair fights. We amuse ourselves and keep busy by making the most of being alive.

However, being confined in the hospital isn't all fun, by any means. My wounds are a long way from being completely healed, and the recovery process is extremely painful. The most agonizing part is when my bandages are changed, which happens twice a day. I have these holes in my body where I was shot, and they are stuffed with gauze to keep them clean of germs and soak up the blood. After a while, the gauze dries out and needs to be changed to prevent infection from setting in. To remove the gauze, the orderlies literally yank it right out of the holes. When they do this, the pain is incredible, maybe more intense than when hit by a bullet. Some soldiers need to be restrained from attacking orderlies who have the responsibility of performing this thankless task.

After two weeks, I am finally beginning to adapt better to my physical difficulties. I'm thankful for this, too, because I hurt without letup and have had to learn to live with all the discomfort. The mere act of scratching an itch can send bolts of pain screaming through my body. It hurts me just to breathe, and the process of urinating causes real agony. Because of my injuries, I am unable to even get up to use a bathroom, so I have a bag attached to my intestines that collects my waste. When I urinate, it burns like crazy, and I need to summon all my self-control to keep from ripping the bag right out of my stomach. But I'm alive, which is what matters, and so whenever the pain seems like more than I can deal with, I try to remember how fortunate I am to eventually be heading home.

—

On June 23, 1968, less than three months after the siege had ended, the Khe Sanh Combat Base was abandoned and razed to the ground by American forces.[1]

June 24, 1968
Journal Entry

I read in today's paper that they closed down Khe Sanh. I know I was only a low-life peon in the Marine Corps, not a general or colonel or other high-ranking officer. To this day, though, I don't understand why they had us remain on that base like sitting ducks, taking that beating, without allowing us to do anything to improve our situation. It seems now that the whole strategy was a waste of personnel and resources, and most importantly, a waste of lives. Those in command confined us to the base and let the North Vietnamese pick us off. And what purpose did it all serve? I'm not sure our presence at Khe Sanh served any military objective. So many of our American boys were killed or seriously injured, and in the end, they just gave the base away. We had the will and the firepower to fight back, but instead we were forced to sit idly by and bide our time, while brave Marines died.

September 29, 1968

The rubber wheels glided smoothly over the linoleum tiles as Dan was rolled through the winding maze of hospital hallways. The nurse stopped the wheelchair just short of the double doors that marked the building's main entrance, and handed Dan his crutches. He stood up with a boost from the crutches, and took several halting steps toward the glass doors. The military truck that would transport him to the airport idled just outside. Almost five long months of slow and painful recovery and rehabilitation had ended.

"Thank you for everything," he said, turning to smile at the nurses who were gathered around to say goodbye. "I would like to say I'll see you again soon, but—"

"That's all right," one of the nurses said, smiling back at Dan. "You take it easy."

"I will," Dan replied as he unceremoniously passed through the double doors and made his way to the waiting military truck.

After sluggishly and cautiously climbing into the cab of the truck, Dan was driven to the airport, where he boarded a military plane that flew him across the Pacific Ocean and then over the breadth of the United States. Landing at McGuire Air Force Base in New Jersey, Dan was immediately shuttled to a hospital at the Philadelphia Naval Base, less than ten miles from where his family lived. He was almost home.

October 8, 1968
Journal Entry

I sat waiting, nervous as hell, in the crowded rec room of the Naval Hospital. After I realized I had no fingernails left to bite, I decided to get up and pace about for as long as my legs could bear. My eyes, when not glancing at the clock on the wall every thirty seconds or so, were fixed on the entrance at the far end of the room. Every time someone entered through the doorway, I tensed in anticipation, hoping it was my family.

Following what felt like an eternity of waiting, the doors swung open and in walked my mom, followed closely by Uncle Jim. My legs felt weak, but somehow I managed to limp halfway across the room, right into my mother's open arms. I wrapped my arms tightly around her, not daring to let go. Tears streamed down her face. She tried to tell me how much she had missed me, but couldn't finish her thought because she had become too overwhelmed to speak coherently. I was also at a loss for words, my throat tied in a huge knot. I was so happy to see my mother again.

After an embrace that seemed to last several minutes, we finally let go of one another, and I turned to Uncle Jim and gave him a great big hug as well. Releasing my hold on Uncle Jim, I went back to hugging my mom. She was thrilled to see me, which was apparent because that's what she kept telling me through her emotional sobs. After she finally settled down, the three of us sat on some folding chairs in a corner of the room and talked. It really didn't matter what we discussed. What did count was that we were with one another. Mom told me that the neighbors couldn't wait to see me, and Uncle Jim got me caught up on the Phillies and mentioned that we would catch a game in the spring if I was feeling up to it. This marked the first time I had seen either of them in over a year, and it felt fantastic to be alive just to see them at all.

Chapter 15

-1968 to 1986-

"I worry that my son might not understand what I've tried to be. And if I were to be killed, Willard, I would want someone to go to my home and tell my son everything. Everything I did, everything you saw. . . . Because there is nothing I detest more than the stench of lies."
    -Marlon Brando as Colonel Kurtz in "Apocalypse Now"

"The tragedy of modern war is that the young men die fighting each other - instead of their real enemies back home in the capitals."
                                            -Edward Abbey

Dan's mother marked the occasion of his official return home by throwing a party, which was attended by virtually all his family and friends. Dan's favorite foods were served, and everyone joyously celebrated his safe return. He chatted briefly with most of the guests, and enjoyed a warm roast beef sandwich and a six-pack of beer. Although it was good to be back in the neighborhood where he was raised, Dan felt out of touch and out of place. As much as he appreciated receiving the attention, he was uncomfortable accepting it.

Needing some time to himself, he eventually made his way outside, unnoticed by family or guests. Then, giving little thought to having walked out on his welcome home party, he hopped on the public transit bus that ran past his house. For the remainder of the evening, Dan rode the same bus back and forth between the Germantown and Frankford sections of Philadelphia, never once considering that he get off when it passed his house. His body molded itself into the seat cushion as he stared out the window, taking in the sights of a city he had not seen in more than a year. By the time Dan finally exited the bus, a driver other than the one who had collected his fare was behind the wheel, and the sun was rising in the early morning sky.

January 21, 1969

"Thank you very much, son," the train conductor said as he took Dan's ticket. The *click, click, click* of the hole-puncher piercing the paper ticket sounded in Dan's ear. "And welcome home," added the conductor.

"Thank you," Dan replied, as he was handed his ticket stub. On his way to Boston to visit family, he was wearing his Marine dress khakis in order to receive a military discount on his fare, a detail obviously not lost on the conductor. Dan placed the stub on the seatback in front of him, and turned to gaze out the window at the passing countryside. After becoming bored with staring at the monotonous streams of industrial parks and traffic on nearby highways, he decided to take a short nap. When he awakened a half-hour later, Dan was almost immediately greeted by words obviously meant to grab his attention. The voice itself was unfamiliar, but the tone and the words being communicated were entirely too familiar.

"So how many people did you kill, man? Huh? How many women and children did you fucking murder?"

Dan looked up through his sleepy daze and shifted his concentration across the aisle to the person speaking. He first observed the scraggly head of long hair bound back by a rainbow-colored headband. Next, he noticed the scruffy beard, and then Dan's eyes fixed on the old, tattered clothing. Finally, he detected a pungent smell, a combination of pot, incense, and days without bathing.

It did not take Dan more than a moment to conclude that while he dozed off, this particular individual had spotted the military uniform and decided to sit down near him for the specific purpose of provoking a confrontation. Having clearly heard the question, Dan glared indignantly at his new neighbor. Dan didn't have any personal grudge against the hippie lifestyle, and respected the right of those living it, or of anyone else, to take sides against the war. However, he was becoming increasingly frustrated with being the object of verbal abuse hurled by those opposed to the involvement of the United States in the Vietnam conflict. This was hardly the first time he had been confronted about having served with the Marines in Vietnam, but he was growing more upset with each passing incident at how brazen and bitter the attacks were progressively becoming, and disheartened by the typically misinformed and slanderous content of the condemnations. It hurt deeply that people were blaming Dan and his fellow grunts for a war over which they had no control or input.

"So how does it feel to be a killer, man?" the protestor asked again.

Instead of reacting violently or even verbally to this line of questioning, Dan took a deep breath, arose from his seat, and proceeded into the next car. He found a vacant aisle seat, and as he sat down, heard the squeaking sound of the train car door opening behind him. Without bothering to turn around, he anticipated he was being followed.

"What's the matter, soldier?" the protestor asked from over his shoulder, this time the voice resonating through the entire car. It was raised considerably louder now, presumably for emphasis, to draw the attention of the other passengers, to make certain that every person in the car would become involved in the face-off. "Aren't you proud about killing all those innocent people?"

As the relentless war protester reached Dan's seat, Dan again stood. Still managing to contain his emotions, he sidestepped his adversary and moved into yet another car. Once more, the hippie followed, this time right on Dan's heels, continuing his malicious tirade. Vehemently offering his opinion on the US involvement in Vietnam for everyone in the train car to hear, he ranted about American baby killers and railed against other atrocities allegedly committed in Vietnam by the violent and ruthless American soldiers.

Heading for the door to the next car, Dan discovered that he had run out of train. With nowhere else to flee from his pursuer, he decided enough was enough—this was where he would make his stand. Stopping in the aisle, he readied to turn around and face his antagonist. But before he could do so, he felt a hand on his shoulder. He turned and looked into the face of a man he had never seen before. Although the person was a complete stranger, Dan knew his type well, and the sense of familiarity helped him to gain some composure. Looking at the weathered lines on the stranger's face, and noticing the American flag pin in his lapel, Dan pictured this person back in the old neighborhood sitting on a porch draped with the Stars and Stripes, a cold beer in hand, reminiscing about World War II.

"Relax, Marine," the stranger said. "I'll take care of this."

"What's your problem, son?" the stranger asked in a low voice as he turned to the hippie. "You think this Marine is a baby killer? A murderer? Is that it? Son, you don't know anything." The hippie took a step backward, realizing he was no longer in charge of the conversation. "You know, this perception that people like you have about the soldiers who have served in Vietnam is completely false. You think that all they do is invade villages and rape and beat civilians, burn down homes, and massacre innocent people. Well, let me tell you something. Those stories are bullshit. They're propaganda, fabricated by cowards such as you. They were invented so that people like you can irresponsibly twist the truth around in order to suit your own personal agendas. Meanwhile, you totally ignore the realities of war."

At that moment, one could have heard a pin drop in the rail car. Every passenger listened intently as the stranger resumed speaking in a calm tone.

"If civilians die in Vietnam, they die by accident. There is a war in Vietnam, and unfortunately stuff like that happens in war. War is brutal. It sucks. But no one I knew or fought alongside of would have stood for the killing of innocent women and children. I'm certain the same goes for those who fought at the side of this Marine here. The guys who fought alongside me were decent and honorable men. I lost lots of good friends in Europe, and I'm sure this Marine lost just as many close buddies in Vietnam. But you don't seem to care much about his friends or their families. Why don't you try worrying about the people who were his friends and died?"

The stranger paused and took a deep breath.

"Now, I'm going to say this one time. If you don't knock it off and go away, you will find out firsthand exactly how violent a Marine can be."

With that, the stranger turned and looked at Dan as the protestor disappeared without further comment. Dan nodded to the stranger in appreciation. The stranger knowingly nodded in return, and like the aging war veteran he was, proudly took his seat. Dan dropped into the closest available seat and turned his attention back to the countryside. Staring out the window, he wondered how much longer it was to Boston.

—

As the war progressed, a growing belief formed among a loud and vocal group of American antiwar protesters that many United States soldiers fighting in Vietnam were committing unspeakable atrocities. One supposition was that soldiers frequently entertained themselves by raping, torturing, or killing Vietnamese civilians, including women and children. This stigma resulted in generalizations being voiced that branded all the American troops as serial rapists and killers. A second assumption categorized the troops as plunderers who stormed into villages, destroyed the crops and livestock, burned the homes, and stole everything of value. To large numbers of antiwar activists, both types of behavior were to be expected, inasmuch as they were of the opinion that our fighting men were inherently deranged. Others among the antiwar zealots held the equally perverted perception that the majority of American troops were simply thugs who used the war to vent their animalistic instincts. The bottom line was that the typical soldier in Vietnam came to symbolize, at least in the eyes of the hard core within the antiwar movement, an evil, violent, morally corrupt killer.

Certainly, there were Americans who committed atrocities in Vietnam, just as there are atrocities perpetrated in every war by all sides. War is a horrible, ugly, violent spectacle that can evoke vile, savage behavior in some people. It was incorrect and irresponsible to claim, as some Americans undertook to do, that unfortunate and regrettable events did not happen in Vietnam. However, it was no less irresponsible for Vietnam War protesters to fire broadsides seeming to accuse every US soldier who fought in Vietnam of plundering villages, raping women, and murdering helpless babies and other non-combatants. Such broad accusations served only to slander the overwhelming majority of American soldiers who remained principled, decent, God-fearing human beings in the face of such tremendous violence. American atrocities were, in truth, isolated events carried out by rogue individuals. Few of the soldiers who fought in Vietnam, including those with whom Dan served, would have tolerated the horrors that so many in the antiwar camp asserted were repeatedly committed by American forces.

Did the killing of innocent civilians occur in Vietnam? Undoubtedly, it did. Wars are repulsive and unfair. When they are fought, people die. Tragically, the wrong people sometimes die. But does that mean the American soldiers who fought in Vietnam, who killed enemy combatants, and who may have also accidentally taken the lives of non-combatants while engaged in the heat of battle, were themselves immoral murderers? Does it follow that they were the depraved animals that a great many antiwar activists made them out to be? In considering

173

the answer to these questions, it is important to first reflect on the identity of the Americans who served in Vietnam.

Today, one can easily identify the typical Vietnam servicemen of forty years ago by simply taking a quick look around his or her own present-day neighborhood or community. Do you know the kid making sandwiches behind the deli counter, helping to prepare breakfast as a short-order cook at your favorite greasy-spoon diner, or serving burgers at a fast food restaurant? How about the kid fixing cars at the neighborhood body shop, working as a stock-boy in the hardware store, or as a check-out clerk at a supermarket, or helping to lay patios or working as an apprentice plumber for a building contractor? Do you know the quarterback on the high school football team? Perhaps you know a youngster who volunteers his time as an assistant coach for a local youth sports team, or works as a lifeguard during the summer at the pool that you frequent. How about the kid who lives down the street from you, who is entering college in the fall? Maybe you have a teenage neighbor who grew up as a friend of one of your own children.

You see these young people driving to the local convenience store to pick up a grocery item at the request of a parent, excited that they are finally old enough to be trusted with the family car. You hear stories from their parents about them going to their prom or out on a date, or you help them load up their family car with cartons packed with clothes and a television set to be transported to their college dorm. Perhaps you have talked politics with one of them who just voted for the first time. You watch them playing for their youth sports team at the neighborhood recreation center, or read about them in the community paper for winning a prize at the high school science fair.

What do all these people have in common? The link is that they are teenagers, young boys, only seventeen or eighteen or nineteen years old. They are still growing up and maturing, hoping to soon become accepted as young adults. You look at these kids, the youth of America, and you may think of them as students, athletes, friends, co-workers, or neighbors, or as sons, brothers, cousins, or uncles.

However, these boys would certainly not conjure up images of cold-blooded killers. You probably could not easily transport them in your mind to a scene of war, locked in battle where ghastly fighting, confusion, and chaos reign. Nor could you even likely be able to picture them manning machine guns, hurling grenades, firing missiles and mortars, or cradling the cold, bloody body of a fallen friend. But if you were to pause for just a moment and consider these kids in a more easily imagined setting, such as one where they are being required to train to fight in a war, you would no doubt be struck by their youth and adolescence.

Having grasped that these youngsters still have much more growing up to do, you might further consider that these very same boys are too young to be handed the kind of responsibilities that combat soldiers must assume. But these are the boys who were among the individuals that our country sent to Vietnam. They were kids, really, who were in most states still too young to purchase alcoholic beverages. They were kids, really, who until the 26th Amendment of the Constitution was ratified in 1971, were not permitted to vote until they turned twenty-one.

They joined the military to serve their country—a goal they thought was honorable and right. They then went to war because they trusted the politicians, who told them they were fighting for the future well-being of the nation, and who they were confident could be relied upon to guide the country on the most beneficial course possible. They were secure in their beliefs, unaware of the mix of influences, pressures, and corruption that can cause those who serve in public office to make bad choices and speak mistruths. And in return for that misplaced trust, thousands of the young servicemen paid with their lives.

Even those who were less trusting, and accordingly questioned the reasons advanced in support of America's involvement in the war, may have found themselves in Vietnam as draftees, unable to bear the consequences of failing to report for military duty. Living with the shame of being labeled a traitor or coward, or ending up in prison, were not options they were willing to choose. And if they were poor, undereducated, or unemployed, without money or prospects, any uncertainties they may have harbored about the war were counteracted by the irresistible pull of the rosy picture painted by the military of a future of thrilling adventures, shiny medals, and money for college tuition.

Whether volunteers or draftees, these American boys could never have been expected to comprehend the horrors of places like Khe Sanh and A Shau. From their homes, schools, and ball fields in communities like Rockland, Maine, Alamogordo, New Mexico, and Ellijay, Georgia, the teens of that time did not have access to CNN or the Internet, or to the general political debate and discourse available to most of today's youth. Instead, they learned about the patriotic virtues of enlisting in the military and the evils of communism in the living rooms, diners, and barbershops of their towns, as conveyed to them by the patriotic, flag-waving men they grew up calling Dad, Uncle, or Coach.

Once they arrived in Vietnam, however, many pondered the likelihood that they were sucked into a war lacking in purpose, and replete with death and destruction, as a result of being duped or fed misleading information. But by then it was too late, so the only possibility for these young soldiers was to fight. They fought not because they were immoral or craved killing and maiming, but for the reason that no other choices were available. By then, there was no turning back. They fought because they wanted to survive. They were too young to die, and they knew it. There were still too many girls to date, future careers to be launched, and achievements to accomplish. They had girlfriends still to marry and families still to start. After all, there are only so many experiences one can fit into a life before the age of eighteen.

Do you remember how you behaved at eighteen? If you were a typical teenager, you were immature and naive, unsure of yourself and your future, still gaining self-confidence, and unprepared for the real world. Who at the age of eighteen could justifiably claim to be ready to face enemy forces in a distant and unfamiliar country, armed with an M-16 and wearing a flak jacket packed with grenades? But this was exactly the situation in which our American boys found themselves. They did their best to fulfill their duty, all the while maintaining the belief that going to Vietnam and performing their military service obligation was the right thing to do. However, they were never sufficiently warned about the brutality that is an element of war. They had little inkling of what they would live through once they arrived in Vietnam. None of these kids gained a clear concept, until their tour was over, of how meaningfully Vietnam would change their lives. In short, they never understood the true hell of war. The only thing these youngsters knew about war, before becoming a participant in one, was that John Wayne always fought on the side that won.

Nonetheless, once they were stuck in Vietnam with no way out, realizing the bleak prospects of their plight, these kids fought with great valor. They had mothers and fathers, brothers and sisters, girlfriends, and other friends and family waiting for them halfway around the world. And so they fought. They would be damned if they were going to return home in flag-draped boxes to the people they cared about, and who cared about them. As would anyone placed in a similar position, they did what they had to do to stay alive.

—

"Whenever I talk with people about Vietnam, one of the questions I always hear is, 'Did you ever kill anyone?' I remember that one of the first things my sister asked me when I got home was, 'So how many people did you kill?' I'm not going to try to kid you. Lots of people were killed in the war. No one kept a scorecard of how many guys they killed, but if you did someone, then everyone knew. When someone got a kill, everyone would walk around proclaiming, 'Hey, good job,' but I didn't feel that way about it. I never felt that way inside because I knew they were still human beings, just like us. My mother raised me by the Ten Commandments, and one of the commandments is 'Thou shalt not kill.' Marines were supposed to lose all compassion for the North Vietnamese, repressing any human feelings we might have had, so when it came time to kill them there would be no hesitation.

I never felt good about the actions we took. But it never had anything to do with agreeing or disagreeing with the politics of the war. Rather, it was about if we didn't do them, they were going to do us. You have to understand that the killing never got personal. It was that they're there, you're here, and you're shooting back and forth. It came down to the basic idea of survival. Most times, I couldn't be sure of what happened because of all the shooting and confusion. There was either too much smoke, it was too dark, or I just simply had my eyes closed out of fear. Mostly, fear and adrenaline controlled the fight. The majority of the time, when I fired my weapon I did it blindly and indiscriminately, and mostly I missed.

For a long time, my son Michael tried to pump me for as much information as he could get from me on this subject. Some stuff, however, I just would not get into with him. I'm not sure if I want my kids to know that I could do something like that to another human being. I don't think I want them to know about that part of my life. I am not sure how they would judge me. When they ask me about Vietnam, I tell them I served in the infantry, that I fought in a war, and that in wars people die, but I won't go any further than that."

—

As if enduring the daily life and death struggle of Vietnam was not enough of a challenge, when our soldiers returned home from the war they were faced with new battles to fight. Unlike what transpired following the wars of their fathers, there were no ticker tape parades to welcome home American troops returning from the battlefields of Vietnam. Instead, the Vietnam returnees watched on television screens or were direct witnesses to an onslaught of well-planned, skillfully orchestrated, and highly visible antiwar demonstrations across the United States.

As the antiwar movement gained support, the soldiers returning from Vietnam became the war's scapegoats. Wounded veterans, many of whom suffered debilitating injuries, were mocked and treated with disrespect and irreverence. It became common for veterans to be subjected to derision in public, and to serve as targets of seething verbal attacks from angry Americans, who would sometimes go so far as to pelt soldiers with garbage and even human excrement. Many who served were prompted, subsequent to being labeled and treated as outcasts and burdened with a sense of shame, to avoid acknowledging their participation in the conflict. For those returnees, the war was best treated as a big secret. Unlike in the case of the wars of their fathers, having fought for their country in Vietnam provided no sense of pride or accomplishment for the returning servicemen.

Antiwar activism was not just confined to public protests. It flourished on a very personal level. Friends, classmates, and even siblings who had not fought in the war, showed contempt for their peers, schoolyard friends, and brothers who had. In the opinion of many veterans, even the government turned its back on those who served. They viewed the level of medical and personal care and treatment provided in Veterans Administration hospitals for recuperating servicemen as totally inadequate, or deficient in critical respects.

Much of the negative attitude directed toward the returning soldiers grew out of the image of the violent and immoral grunt in Vietnam that had become ingrained in the minds of many misinformed Americans. Part of the misconception was founded upon an interest in stopping the war by any means necessary, even if the antiwar movement relied upon creating and cultivating false perceptions. As a result, protesters would shape their own truths for their own advantages, regardless of the consequences. In some instances, the negative reaction flowed from protesters directing the anger and hatred they held for the inaccessible politicians and military leadership toward the more visible and accessible enlisted servicemen.

Another significant reason for the disapproving attitude toward Vietnam veterans, when compared to veterans of previous American wars, was the inordinate amount of exposure that immoral behavior received in the media, relative to its actual level of occurrence. While there can be no doubt that atrocities were committed by Americans, they were random and isolated events. Nonetheless, these actions usually became front-page news. On the other hand, very little fanfare was ever made of North Vietnamese and Viet Cong atrocities, which occurred on a much greater and more methodical scale. While there are documented cases of US atrocities, there is overwhelming evidence that the North Vietnamese and Viet Cong engaged in a pattern of brutality and executions of civilians during the war. Who has not heard of the horrible atrocities committed by Americans at My Lai? However, what do most Americans know about the NVA's and Viet Cong's systematic approach to torture and mass execution, which the North pursued in an attempt to force South Vietnamese civilians to support the communist war effort?

For example, the city of Hue was the sight of several horrific atrocities. At the tomb of Tu Duc and Dong Khanh, an unearthed mass grave revealed 201 civilian victims who had been either shot in the back of the head or buried alive.[1] During the TET offensive, the North Vietnamese organized the execution of over 1,000 of the city's civilian residents.[2] And several mass graves uncovered near the city contained South Vietnamese civilians who had been shot and then buried up to their necks, so that when the bodies were found their faces were unrecognizable due to animals eating away at the exposed flesh.[3]

In the town of Ap Dong Gi, the bodies of one hundred South Vietnamese civilians were found after they were buried alive. In Ban Me Thout, Viet Cong rebels killed six United States missionaries working at a leprosarium and then booby-trapped their dead bodies.[4] Another fourteen American civilians were slaughtered by the NVA while working at a pacification program in South Vietnam.[5] Also slain were four United Nations priests, two French Benedictine monks, and two French priests.[6]

The purpose of these brief examples of enemy atrocities committed during the Vietnam War is not an attempt to deflect criticism of American atrocities, nor are they meant to compare the behavior of Americans with that of the North Vietnamese or Viet Cong to minimize the wrongful actions of rogue US troops. Rather, they are intended to reinforce the point that American troops should not have been made the whipping boys for those who were ideologically opposed to US involvement in Vietnam, by underscoring the principle that war will always be war, and neither side in the Vietnam conflict could escape this reality.

Of course, many of the Americans who protested the Vietnam conflict had somehow avoided the draft or otherwise circumvented military service. Putting aside the politics of their decision to not serve, most of these protesters, as a consequence of their lack of combat experience, simply did not comprehend the realities of what the American armed forces faced in Vietnam. The great majority of war protesters typically knew little of the truth about the war. They had no perception about the reality of the harsh conditions under which American soldiers lived, and the deceit that was woven into the indoctrination period preceding a soldier's arrival in Vietnam. They had no concept of what it meant to fight for one's own survival. They did not understand how the soldiers, when confronted with the choice of either living or dying, which sometimes involved having to decide between right and wrong, did what human nature dictated: They fought to live another day.

More than 58,000 American men and women died in Vietnam.[7] Hundreds of thousands more were wounded, many permanently debilitated by their injuries. Our young boys died by the thousands in Vietnam, but that consequence of the war seemed to escape consideration by those who were never there to witness the hostilities. It is upsetting to contemplate that those individuals who claimed to love every living human being could not generate positive feelings or a show of support for their own friends, children, and brothers who served.

In addition to the physical wounds, thousands of those who survived Vietnam suffered post-traumatic stress disorders that rendered them incapable of functioning normally in their daily lives. But the protesters were not sensitive to this issue, either. They wanted to end the war, yet in their frenzy to do so, ignored the impact of their anti-Vietnam War activities on the psyche of returning troops. And so, perhaps as a result of naiveté, frustration, or blind anger, instead of trying to understand the predicament into which others misled so many of our soldiers, the protesters simply ostracized our boys due to their involvement in the war. In the struggle to purge the war germ from the American body politic, the protesters contributed significantly to the pain of our troops.

More members of the military who fought in Vietnam were inflicted with post-traumatic stress than in any other war in our country's history. It is not unreasonable to surmise that a major reason for this outcome was the lack of support, and outright hostility, that our soldiers received from the American public as they arrived home. This aggression, mockery, and resentment directed at the troops following their homecoming from Vietnam, coupled with the challenges of assimilating back into society while recovering from psychological war wounds, proved just as devastating to many veterans as the horrors they actually experienced in battle.

Looking back on the contemptible reception received by our servicemen, it is difficult to understand why protesters of the Vietnam War were not more supportive of the returnees. Granted, war is an abomination, and protest can prove essential in helping to bring specific armed conflicts to an end. However, the fact that a vast number of Americans angrily directed their dissenting views regarding our involvement in the Vietnam War at the soldiers who fought in the trenches represents a shameful, embarrassing blemish on this country's history.

The years during which the Vietnam conflict raged were turbulent times in America's annals, but it is important that we never lose sight of the factors that created the environment in which our troops found themselves. America's politicians and military establishment sent our young boys to a country that hardly any of those youngsters knew much about, for reasons very few of them understood. It was not a battle of the soldiers' choosing. Rather, they were drawn into a war under a complicated and confusing set of political circumstances. Thousands sacrificed their lives, limbs, and mental health in the belief that America's freedom was in some way at stake. Their reward for this show of patriotism and service to their country was to be spit-on, screamed at, shunned, and labeled "baby-killers." Somehow, it seems, our servicemen deserved better.

Hopefully, future generations of Americans will have the courage, decency, and respect to support all the members of our armed forces in the event they should ever again have to shoulder the burden of fighting to survive a "politicians'" war.

March 15, 1969
Dan walked with a deliberate, unhurried gait to the front entrance of the Philadelphia Naval Base and then stopped. He took a drag on his cigarette and turned around to catch a final glimpse of the base. He was not sure exactly why he sought one last glance, though he considered several possible reasons. For one, he was about to walk out of the Marine Corps forever, and this would be his last look back on military life. In light of his injuries, Dan had today received his honorable discharge papers and was released from any further military obligation. In a few moments, when he stepped beyond the Naval Base perimeter, he would officially become a civilian again.

Or maybe Dan turned around hoping to see one of his many friends, such as Robbie or Lance or Jimmy, who he had left behind in Vietnam. He missed his friends as much today as ever before. They had been through so much together that at times Dan felt empty without them around. It was difficult never having had an opportunity to say goodbye to any of them. He prayed that those still alive when he was wounded had managed to stay safe, and that any who had not made it were now in a better place. His greatest regret was that he could not have done more to help all of them return home safely to their loved ones.

Or possibly Dan was waiting for someone he did not know. Perhaps, if he stood there long enough, an officer covered in brass would approach him, maybe a colonel or even a general with stars pinned to his jacket. Maybe he was hoping to bump into a politician, like a US senator or member of the US House of Representatives, or a ranking member of the White House staff. He would be satisfied to encounter anyone who had played any sort of role in resolving to send Dan and his friends off to the jungles of Vietnam to fight a war while that individual remained to the rear of the battle zone, or even stateside, all the while dressed up in medals or playing political games.

Perhaps Dan paused because he hoped that any chance encounter would result in the other person saying, "Thank you." Maybe that was all Dan was looking for. Someone to say, "Thank you. Thank you, son.

Thank you for putting your life on the line. Thank you for fighting for your country. Thank you for living in filth and squalor, without sufficient food and water, and in constant fear. Thank you for watching while so many of your friends died or were maimed for life. Thank you for being shot five times, and I hope you don't have too much difficulty adjusting to the mental and physical scars. Thank you for performing a job well done, and good luck in the future."

But in the end, as Dan stepped gingerly off the curb and onto the street, there were no friends to greet, no chance encounters, and no heartfelt expressions of thanks. Instead, he took leave of the United States Marine Corps with nothing but the free haircut that he had received earlier in the morning.

The 1970s

Shortly after coming home to Philadelphia, Dan attempted to bring some direction to his life, enrolling at Temple University on the GI Bill. However, after only two classes, Dan was reminded of what he had already been aware before joining the Marines, namely that college was not for him. After dropping out of Temple, Dan had no idea of what to do with himself or what direction to take regarding a vocation. Most of his waking hours were spent loafing around the house or hanging out in the neighborhood, usually with a beer in his hand. He drank almost every day now, and the cycle of drinking was wearing on his mother.

Using money saved from working the occasional odd job, Dan bought a motorcycle and rode to California to stay with a buddy from Vietnam. He accomplished little in California, mostly goofing off. Several months later, having run out of money, he sold his bike and used the proceeds to pay for a bus ticket back to Philadelphia.

Back from Vietnam for almost two years, Dan was now drinking heavily. He still had only a high school education to depend upon, and despite his initial expectations formed when he entered the Marine Corps, he was never trained to perform any marketable work skills. Dan figured he could parlay the combat experience he acquired as a Marine into a career as a stick-up man, but no way in hell was he allowing himself to head down that road. And so, while Dan tried to figure out what to do with his life, he drank.

As the months passed, it became clear that the war had inflicted severe mental trauma on Dan that was excruciatingly slow to heal. At night, he would often awaken abruptly from his sleep in the midst of a nightmare, jumping out of bed screaming. Breathing deeply and trying to regain his composure, Dan would find himself dripping with sweat and shivering. When he first began to exhibit this type of conduct, his mother would come dashing into his room in an attempt to provide a calming presence. But the nightmares about the war persisted, and as the episodes turned more violent, Dan's mother became too frightened of her own son to enter his room while he was in this mental state.

The haunting memories of the war had other impacts on Dan's behavior patterns. He lived in a state of paranoia, distrustful of everyone, including his own friends and family. He carried his .45 with him wherever he went, even if only to the corner grocery, and always slept with it under his pillow. Dan felt safer having a weapon with him at all times. He figured some habits die hard.

Dan recognized he was becoming a burden to his mother, and was fully aware that it was time to find a steady occupation. He visited the VA, who helped place him in a position in the shipping department of a medical parts supplier. Dan disliked the idea of working in a factory, but knew he needed to clean up his act and earn some money. Nonetheless, he continued to drink when not working or sleeping. As his distaste for the job grew, it was becoming obvious to him that he would not continue to work in a factory forever. But compelled to maintain some sense of responsibility, Dan resisted the urge to quit, thus causing the boredom and depression brought on by employment in a factory setting to draw him deeper into his pit of despair. To make matters worse, the one stabilizing presence in his life, his mother, was becoming increasingly upset and impatient with Dan's living style.

While in this state of stagnation, Dan met a young woman named Caitlin, in whom he developed a romantic interest. After a short romance, they married in 1973 and moved into their own place. They had two children together, Brandon and Megan. However, the marriage ended in divorce after just a few years, although it was really all but over after a matter of months. Dan's emotional condition made it impossible for their marriage to stand any chance of success. Much of the time, Dan found himself in a depressed state, and the nightmares that interrupted his sleep still occurred with great frequency. Obsessed with memories of Vietnam, virtually every waking thought was in some regard connected to the war. The memories were controlling his life. And when the recollections of the horrific images were not causing emotional pain, or contributing to feelings of overwhelming guilt and remorse for leaving behind fallen friends, he would become severely distressed over the manner in which people treated him as a returning vet.

To further intensify his problems, Dan's drinking escalated as his marriage dissolved, and his frustrations mounted over his unsuccessful search for a method to combat his emotional demons. Regularly drinking a half-case of beer each night, he fell into a comfortable routine of going to work in the morning and returning home in the evening to drink. On the weekends, there was no work to impede his drinking.

Shortly after the divorce became final, Dan was flipping through a newspaper and spotted an advertisement seeking applicants for the Philadelphia police force. Frustrated with a history of working at low-paying and inconsequential jobs, and tired of his dead-end lifestyle, a job as a police officer certainly held some appeal. Dan obtained and then submitted an application, and shortly thereafter took written and physical tests, both of which he passed. However, because of the wounds he suffered in Vietnam, Dan was initially denied admission into the Philadelphia Police Academy.

Not willing to abandon his pursuit of a position in law enforcement, Dan persisted in his attempts to gain acceptance to the police department's training program. His tenacity was finally rewarded when he was admitted to the academy in 1976. There was now a bona fide reason for him to give up drinking, and his outlook on life turned positive. With a goal to guide him and a hopeful future in sight, Dan began training for his new career. Successfully completing the training course became the dominating motivational force in his life. Remarkably, after years of heavy drinking, Dan remained sober throughout the entirety of the academy program. He also managed to push his thoughts about the war into the back of his mind. Six months later, he proudly graduated, and was sworn in as a Philadelphia police officer. Finally, it appeared Dan was on the right track. However, without the constant training to occupy his time, he once again found himself ruminating about the war and struggling to remain sober.

One evening, after an uneventful day shift on a robbery detail, Dan and several other officers with whom he was working headed to a nightclub in downtown Philadelphia. Dan had been serving as a police officer for almost three years, his drinking was relatively under control, and life seemed to be looking up for him, notwithstanding his tendency to dwell on the past if his mind was not occupied with work.

Standing at the bar with his police buddies, something inexplicable prompted Dan to turn around and focus his attention across the room. There stood a woman who struck his eye. Uncharacteristically, Dan walked over to her and introduced himself. Her name was Gloria, and the two of them spent the rest of the evening talking, their conversation carrying over into the early morning, long after the other customers had drifted out of the bar. After last call, they continued chatting over breakfast at an all-night diner. Two years later they were married.

The early 1980s

Gloria and Dan's first son, Michael, was born in 1980. Dan loved and adored his family, and along with a job in a profession in which he took pride, there was reason for optimism that he might be on the verge of breaking free from his past.

Soon after Michael was born, however, Dan started to suffer from fits of depression. He found himself spending more of his time reflecting on Vietnam and drinking steadily again. Though he never once showed up for work as a police officer with as much as a single beer in his system, he tended to exhibit less self-control when off-duty.

One of the major triggers that precipitated Dan's newest bout with depression was the American hostage crisis in Iran. He was deeply agitated by the groundswell of support the hostages received, as well as the outpouring of concern over their well-being, sentiments few seemed to share for Vietnam veterans. Not that the welfare of the hostages wasn't important, and not that people shouldn't have had them in their thoughts and prayers, but where was this concern for Dan and his fellow veterans? The Iranian hostage crisis served to underscore the lack of national sympathy received by the Vietnam veterans. It highlighted, at least for Dan, the insufficient amount of attention being paid to the plight of the many Vietnam veterans who were now unemployed, unsuccessfully dealing with war-related stress, addicted to alcohol or drugs, or displaying one of the many other mental or physical side effects of having served in the war or arising from the transition to civilian life. Where was the outpouring of empathy for those veterans who were now having trouble coping with life? Dan saw none, and that both frustrated and angered him. These emotions, in turn, evolved into depression.

In 1983, Gloria gave birth to the couple's second son, Robert. While Dan was briefly lifted out of his despair by this happy event, he soon found himself again battling depression. Eventually, his depression reached a level where it caused him to withdraw inwards, the mental pain having pushed Dan to the point where, except for going to work, he would not leave the house. He rarely spoke with Gloria, hardly interacted with his children, and found himself obsessing about the war. Rightfully worried and upset by Dan's behavior, Gloria tried to help him work through the issues and problems that had plagued him for nearly fifteen years. After much pleading, Gloria convinced him to go to a Veterans Administration hospital for counseling. The VA doctors diagnosed Dan as suffering post-traumatic stress syndrome, as well as what was termed "survivor's guilt." According to the medical findings, Dan was haunted by the fact that he survived Vietnam, but so many of his buddies had died there. As a result, he was overwhelmed with feelings of guilt, which stemmed from a belief that he let down those who died by not doing enough to protect and save them.

Dan began to receive counseling for these diagnoses, but his relationship with Gloria did not improve, and the therapy assisted only minimally in other respects. As much as she pleaded with Dan to intensify his efforts at working with the psychologists, Gloria was met by resistance and scorn. Dan was too wrapped up in his own self-pity to see that she was trying her best to help him. Then, in 1985, after five years of struggling exhaustively to be as supportive as possible, Gloria's patience wore out and she left, taking Michael and Rob with her. Gloria and Dan were divorced shortly thereafter.

With Gloria gone, the depression and drinking worsened. Not long after Gloria moved away, Steve Nichols, one of Dan's good friends from Vietnam, with whom he had kept in close contact, moved into the house. While the two were good friends, Steve, like Dan, maintained a destructive lifestyle. This made living together a strenuous arrangement. In addition, although Steve himself did not use drugs, he hosted parties that were often loud and disorderly and to which guests, both invited and uninvited, frequently brought illegal drugs. Aside from the conflict this presented to Dan in light of his professional responsibilities, Dan understood that if drugs were ever found in his home, he would most certainly lose his job and possibly face criminal charges. Therefore, although it pained Dan to do so, he eventually asked Steve to move out.

Then, one summer night in 1986, Dan decided he had endured enough.

♠

Chapter 16

-1986: Part II-

"The horror! The horror!"

-Joseph Conrad, "Heart of Darkness"

Dan opened his eyes. A lone tear streamed down his cheek. He was not sure how much time had elapsed while he sat on the couch, contemplating the ups and downs of his life, but he was certain it had been quite a while. He listened to the sound of the cars passing outside, and felt the cool summer breeze blow through the open windows of his living room and against the sweat covering his face. Almost twenty years had passed, but the memories of his experiences in Vietnam were still vivid and haunting, constantly reminding him of what he lived through during the war. Dan placed the virtually empty bottle of beer onto the table, lit a cigarette, and began to cry. He buried his face in his hands and released every tear that had been trapped behind the anger and depression that had consumed him for years.

Dan badly needed a friend in whom he could confide, so he nervously reached for the telephone and called Steve Nichols, with whom he had periodically remained in contact since Steve had moved out. Steve arrived at Dan's home within minutes, and the two friends talked briefly about Dan's sense of desperation. Steve then embarked on a mission of mercy through the house, collecting Dan's guns, including the one in the basement, and emptying all the liquor and beer into the kitchen sink. Dan and Steve then sat and smoked cigarettes through the night, while Dan calmed himself and struggled to regain his composure. When Steve left in the morning, Dan's hands were no longer shaking, and his heartbeat was returning to normal. Dan knew it was time to start over, to stop the drinking, and to get his life in order. He would start that day.

♠

Chapter 17

-Epilogue-

*"Have you ever been close to tragedy,
or been close to folks who have?
Have you ever felt a pain so powerful, so heavy you collapse?
Have you ever had the odds stacked up so high,
you need a strength most don't possess?
Or has it ever come down to do or die?
You've got to rise above the rest.
Well, I've never had to, knock on wood, but I know someone who
has, which makes me wonder if I could.
It makes me wonder if, I've never had to,
knock on wood, and I'm glad I haven't yet.
Because I'm sure it isn't good.
That's the impression that I get."*
  -The Mighty Mighty Bosstones, "The Impression That I Get."

"Praised are you, lord our God, king of the universe, for granting us life, for sustaining us, and for helping us reach this day."
                - Jewish prayer

The story related in this book is not meant to elicit debate on whether a vital national interest was protected by placing American soldiers in harm's way in Vietnam. Nor is it about the "domino theory," or whether fighting the war in Vietnam was essential to the free world's struggle to stem the tide of communism. And although the story uses war as a backdrop, it is not intended as a war story. Neither is its intent to serve as a narrative of certain events of the Vietnam conflict, or of the exploits of our military personnel who were there. And it does not have as a purpose to preach about the immorality of war, or to delve into the emotions generated by war and its outcomes. Rather, this story is about the life of Danny Sullivan.

Dan's life is symbolic of the lives of numerous American soldiers whose destinies were forever changed by the Vietnam War. It is a life of a man who has endured trials far beyond what any fair-minded person would expect another individual to have to bear. However, there is far more to Dan's story than a tale meant to elicit feelings of sympathy, shock, and indignation. It is also a narrative about survival, followed by a remarkable turnaround. It is about the triumph that one man achieved when he wiped the image of a .45 from his mind, discovered hope and a second chance, and attained self-redemption and renewal. Finally, Dan's story speaks to the inspiration that should be generated in each of us, upon reading its account, to find our inner-strength as well as to develop the capability to appreciate all of life's many wonders.

The seed from which this book grew was first planted on a warm, sunny, late spring afternoon in 1995. At the time, I was eighteen and just completing my senior year in high school. On that particular day, I was involved in my volunteer role as an assistant coach for the Cubs, my then eleven-year-old brother's youth baseball team. Prior to that day, I had not ever thought to explore in detail any aspect of world history, and I certainly never imagined becoming immersed in examining the Vietnam War era.

At the age of eighteen, not having been born until 1977, I was only vaguely familiar with what had occurred in America during the 1960s and 1970s. I knew little about the assassinations of Robert Kennedy and Martin Luther King Jr., the student protests at Kent State University and the turmoil in the streets of Chicago during the 1968 Democratic National Convention, or the race riots that scarred Los Angeles, Detroit, Newark, and many other cities. I could claim only a slight understanding of the role musicians such as the Beatles, Rolling Stones, and Bob Dylan, or concerts such as Woodstock and the Monterey Pop Festival, had played in shaping that generation of Americans. I never experienced the agony or fervor of our country over the US having become involved in the Vietnam War. And I hardly related to that generation, a population inundated by passionate appeals for peace and exposed to unprecedented experimentation with sex and drugs. But my world would change profoundly on that beautiful spring afternoon in 1995 as I stood on a baseball field located in a quiet neighborhood in the northwest section of Philadelphia.

Dan was also an assistant coach of the Cubs, and it just so happened that his youngest son, Rob, played on the team. On that particular day, Dan and I found ourselves in right field, providing fielding practice to a group of Cubs players roaming around in center field. As Dan whacked fly balls and I shagged throws from the players returning the hit balls, an old military plane buzzed noisily overhead. He and I watched it fly over the field, and then he turned toward me and casually commented, "You know, Ari, one of the first times I flew in a plane like that, I jumped out of it."

When this conversation occurred, I had known Dan for approximately four years. During that period, he had coached both a basketball and baseball team on which I played in a northwest Philadelphia community youth sports organization. When I became too old to play senior league baseball, Dan had asked me to help coach his teams, which eventually led me to join the coaching staff of the Cubs as part of a senior class community service project sponsored by my high school.

During the years I played on his teams, and subsequently served as an assistant coach, I came to appreciate Dan as one of the most caring and generous people I had ever met. He spent hours upon hours coaching as many as three youth sports teams during the same sports season, including the teams on which his two younger sons played. A patient coach who very rarely expressed or displayed anger during the course of a game, he almost never raised his voice when speaking either to players or to umpires or referees. Dan was also a fair coach who always made sure each of his players received the opportunity to participate in every game, no matter what the score or the significance of the game's final outcome.

I witnessed Dan's first-class character on numerous other occasions, as well. For example, he always willingly and graciously provided players a ride to or from the games when their parents were unavailable, typically piling half a dozen kids into the back of his pick-up truck. He enjoyed engaging his players in friendly challenges to see who could make a shot from half-court, or if he could strike them out during batting practice. And he never failed to offer any youngster by his side a soda or hot dog from the snack bar, regardless of whether he intended to get something for himself.

While these are just a few brief examples, they exemplify why Dan, to me, stood in stark contrast to the typical role model I found on the athletic field. He became someone I admired due to his easygoing and friendly manner, and because when I looked into his eyes, I saw a glimmer of goodness that seemed unusual in our cynical, fast-paced, me-first world.

Notwithstanding that I was present on previous occasions when Dan discussed his work with the Philadelphia Police Department, and although I knew by the bumper sticker on his truck that he had served as a Marine, his shy reference to his parachute jump during advanced training in 1967 marked the first instance I had heard him comment on his military service. As he continued to hit fly balls, we started talking about his involvement in the Vietnam War. I do not remember the exact specifics of the conversation, but I vividly recall that within a few minutes I became totally absorbed. What intrigued me most about Dan's recounting of some of his military experiences was that, having recently celebrated my eighteenth birthday, I realized I was then the same age as Dan was when he was sent to Vietnam. Immediately struck by the coincidence, I began trying to picture myself in his shoes almost thirty years earlier when he was eighteen. For the first time, I found myself gaining a real perspective of what it would mean for me to be faced with the prospect of military duty. As I thought about what I considered the major matters then facing me in life—girls, grades, parties, and making sure I was up to date on the latest trends in fashion and music—it occurred to me how trivial these issues were in comparison to those needing to be addressed by individuals engaged in, or soon to be drawn into, military combat.

The mere idea of me having to deal with what Dan had lived through at eighteen was unimaginable. Not in my wildest dreams could I picture myself fighting in any war at the age of eighteen. I recognized that, at eighteen, so many goals and expectations lay ahead of me. To fill my eighteen-year-old mind with the violence and terror Dan confronted in Vietnam struck me as unthinkable. To teach me, as an eighteen-year-old, to kill, or to cause me to be placed in a situation that might result in my death, seemed so insane. As I learned more about Dan's wartime experiences, I could not picture being required at my age to confront the misery, devastation, and human toll that had marked his tour in Vietnam. I began to imagine how I, as an eighteen-year-old, might convey to others the drama and consequences of Dan being thrown into battle at that age.

Over the next several months, I came to gain a deeper understanding of what Dan had undergone in his life, both during and after his service in Vietnam. My perceptions of why I was motivated to write a story about him began to expand as my view of Dan, the person, took on a powerful new dimension.

I had always known Dan to be a nice person, but as I listened to him talk into a tape recorder as we sat at the kitchen counter in my parents' home, I gained an even greater appreciation for the quality of his character. I now respected him not just because of the positive personal qualities that I observed in him, but also on the basis that he somehow managed, despite everything, to retain any positive attributes at all. I began to obtain a clearer picture of the terrible events and experiences through which he had persevered, and of the hell he had endured. Once I placed into the mix the fact of his survival, his peaceful disposition, his kindness, and the manner in which he turned around his life, it became obvious to me that Dan's story made for more than a riveting action narrative. It also served to depict the triumph of an individual over unfathomable adversity.

At some point after his return from Vietnam, Dan had essentially given up any expectation of overcoming his alcohol addiction or the anger and depression that consumed him. He had given up on trying to find a solution to the emotional anguish brought about by the frightful lingering memories of the many traumatic events he experienced in Vietnam. Add to those factors the enduring post-traumatic stress and the ongoing public ostracism to which the Vietnam vets were subjected, and the result was a life almost too unbearable to live. Dan's spirit had died long before 1986. His physical death would be just a formality. But then came that fateful summer night, when Dan found himself alone on his living room couch. Had he decided to surrender, the pain and suffering would have been over. Instead, he chose to make a different decision. It was a choice that required more strength and courage than he had ever exhibited in his life. Admirably, he chose to stand tall on that decisive night and confront life. No longer would he hide from his past behind a bottle. He would challenge himself to confront his anger and depression. He would move into the future by facing life head-on and making the best of what it dealt him.

And so Dan fought back. Not long after the eventful night on which he picked up the phone and called Steve Nichols, thus turning his mind away from his preoccupation with death, life began to change for the better. Finally, after a nearly twenty-year downward slide, there was genuine justification for hope.

One day, in the early fall of 1986, Dan received a phone call from Gloria at his home in the Germantown section of Philadelphia. She explained that her car was broken down, and wondered if he could help. Dan dropped everything and drove to meet her. As Dan finished working on the car, he and Gloria began to catch up with each other. Dan told her he was bringing order back into his life, that he was undergoing therapy to control his anger and conquer his depression, and that he had finally managed to stop drinking. He also admitted to a number of mistakes that had contributed to difficulties in their marriage, and said that he missed her and the children. This conversation marked a new, positive point in the couple's relationship. Gloria and Dan reconciled soon thereafter, and remarried in 1988.

Back with Gloria, Dan's relationship with his two younger children strengthened. He also made an effort to reach out to his two older children and begin the process of healing and rebuilding his relationship with them. In order to spend more time with Michael and Rob, Dan began volunteering as a youth sports coach. He was doing well at work, and had received a promotion to the rank of detective in the Philadelphia Police Department's sex crimes unit. When not on the job, Dan could usually be found at home with his family, or giving selflessly of himself coaching. And he had now successfully remained sober for several years.

As he became more devoted to coaching, Dan proved to be tireless, coaching up to three teams during each basketball and baseball season. For numerous hours each week during the winter, spring, and summer months, Dan attempted to develop the athletic skills of his players. Under no illusions that he was a great sports tactician, Dan coached for the fun of it, and because it made him feel good about himself due to his belief that he was serving an important role in the community. Coaching nourished his sense of purpose in working with children, and he relished being able to spend more time with Michael and Rob.

But Dan's style of coaching evolved from more than just a love of sports and his desire to spend more time with his two youngest sons.

The manner in which he carried himself on the field was a reflection of his overall attitude toward life, an attitude shaped significantly by the number of hard lessons he learned because of Vietnam. In the heat of battle and during the years of reflection that followed, Dan came to appreciate that life is too short and precious to waste on incivility, or to attempt navigating with a closed mind or in too serious a manner.

I learned many lessons from Dan during my years of being associated with his teams, both as a player and coach. One of the most important he taught me was that the outcome of sporting events should not be taken so seriously as to create negative emotions. In turn, he helped me, a young sports fanatic, place into perspective the importance of athletics relative to life's more consequential issues. Though I never heard him explicitly make the point, winning was not one of Dan's top priorities. He was primarily concerned with sportsmanship, perseverance, hustle, and teamwork. Dan certainly did not win all the games he coached in his life, but whether he won or lost, he always strived to build the character of his players. In Dan's eyes, if children walked off the field or court better people, they were winners, regardless of the final score.

By taking the time to listen to Dan's story, not only did I become deeply impressed by the strength he exhibited in facing and overcoming his past, I also discovered a source of inspiration to help guide my own life. I have since been motivated to find my personal inner strength and develop the characteristic of never giving up in the face of adversity without first exerting my very best effort. And in my view, Dan's remarkable story should inspire all those who learn of it to strengthen their determination to persevere whenever faced with a problem of seemingly overwhelming proportions.

Furthermore, Dan's story is one that should remind us to appreciate the greatness of our life here on earth. With every breath we take, we should be inspired to live life to the fullest, in awe of the miracles that surround us. From my own perspective, life is an experience and opportunity that I no longer take for granted, and I have grown to value every day and moment as a gift. As for those instances when I become flustered or overwhelmed by relatively trivial or insignificant problems, and neglect to be grateful for all that life has provided me, or even perhaps engage in self-pity, I try to redirect my thoughts and reflect on the valuable lessons I learned from Dan. Ultimately, knowing that Dan came out on top in the face of all the adversity he has endured, I am steadfast in the conviction that there should be nothing within reason that I too cannot accomplish, if only I set my mind to it.

I do not believe that many of the people who have known Dan realize the full significance of what he has achieved in his lifetime. Most of his friends and acquaintances probably see a caring father who has spent many hours teaching children about basketball and baseball, and a person who established a reputation as a dedicated law enforcement officer. It is unlikely that they are aware of the man who went all the way to the brink, and then returned to society on the back of his inner strength. They most likely know little of the man who overcame the greatest of odds by surviving the physical challenge of staying alive in Vietnam as a teenager, and then confronting and fighting his own demons during the tumultuous years that followed.

And therein lies Dan's triumph. Instead of letting his life experiences destroy him, he prevailed over the adversity he faced and grew into a person who deserves not only our respect, but also our admiration.

I am honored to know Daniel J. Sullivan, and to be able to call him my friend.

It was the early summer of 1999 as I paced back and forth in the third base coach's box, occasionally straying out of the box and walking along the third base foul line. The bases were loaded with two outs in the bottom half of the final inning, and our team, the White Sox, was losing by one run. It was the second game of a best of three playoff series, and we had already lost the first game. If we lost today, we went home, and our season was over. Meanwhile, our opponents, the Padres, would advance to play for the thirteen and fourteen-year-old league baseball championship. If we won, we would stay alive and play the third and final game of the series tomorrow. The hitter who would be faced with the challenge of trying to win the game for the White Sox was Robert Sullivan, who, bat in hand, appeared terrified as he moved toward home plate. It was, I supposed, the reaction to be expected of any thirteen-year-old faced with such a critical at-bat.

Dan Sullivan, the White Sox head coach, stood just outside the entrance to the chain-link batting cage, not more than fifteen feet from home plate. He stole a quick glance at his ever-present clipboard, and then surveyed the field to assess the situation. Rob backed away from home plate, gripped the bat tighter in his hands, and took a deep breath in an effort to calm his nerves. Perhaps sensing his son's anxiety, Dan asked the umpire for a time out. I quickly trotted toward home plate to listen to the advice offered by the stoic head coach. Dan stepped through the entrance of the cage, shouted a few words of instruction to the three runners on base, and turned to Rob, who was moving away from the plate and closer to his dad to better hear his words.

"Look at me," Dan calmly said to his son. "Just relax and stroke the ball."

Rob, not one to talk much under any circumstances, looked up at his dad and simply nodded. He then turned and reentered the batter's box, and I hustled back to my position beside the third base bag.

Back in the coach's box, I yelled at the three runners on base, making certain they each knew what to do if the ball was put into play. I turned to our bench and called out to our team to shout encouragement to Rob. I was nervous as hell, perhaps more so than Rob, if that was possible.

Then I glanced at Dan. His body language and overall manner gave the impression that we were playing the second inning of a meaningless game. I found a bit of peace in his cool demeanor, and so I relaxed a little. I smiled. I let out a small chuckle and decided to just let the baseball gods do their work.

The opposing pitcher wound up and threw the first pitch.

Strike one.

Ball one.

Ball two.

Strike two.

The count was even. I crossed my fingers. The pitcher wound up and delivered the next pitch. Rob, a left-handed hitter, swung and made contact with the ball, pushing a low hard-hit line drive down the third base line, only feet in front of where I was standing. The ball passed so close to me I could have reached down and caught it. The third baseman, who was playing away from third base to adjust for a left-handed hitter, waved weakly at the ball as it hit the infield dirt five feet past the third base bag and bounced into leftfield.

Our bench erupted in celebration, as did the parents sitting in the bleachers behind our team. The ball, now caught up in the thick outfield grass, rolled slowly into shallow left field and came to a stop. By the time the left fielder reached the ball, Rob was standing on second base with a wide grin on his face, and the tying and winning runs had scored. Eighteen games into the season, and it was Rob's first extra-base hit of the year.

The game was over. The White Sox players, forgetting for the moment that they still had a game to play the following day, converged on home plate to mob each other as though they had won the series. Rob began jogging in from second base with the same huge smile still etched on his face. It had been his most important at-bat of the season, and he had come through in the clutch with flying colors.

I met up with Rob as he reached the pitcher's mound, where he was briefly mobbed by his teammates who had come out to greet him. After I expressed a quick word of congratulations to Rob, which he shyly accepted, the two of us headed back to the bench together. Dan was still standing near the opening to the batting cage, celebrating with his players as they lined up at home plate to shake hands with their opponents.

"Hey, Dan," I said as I approached, happier for him than for the White Sox players. "That was your kid who just won us the game."

He kind of shrugged, and then a faint smile crossed his face.

"Hey, thanks, man," he said as we shook hands. "Good game."

After everything he had been through over the years, it was moments like this for which Dan lived.

He then turned to the hero of the game and extended his hand for a big high-five. His next words were spoken through a grin that stretched ear to ear.

"Good job, Robbie."

In 1999, Dan and Gloria again parted ways. As a result, his life has been marked by additional complications, but he retains a positive outlook about the future and a close and loving relationship with all four of his children. He continues to live in the Philadelphia area, where he remains gainfully employed and actively involved as a youth sports coach. He still roots for the Phillies.

A Word of Explanation:

As noted in Chapter 17, the idea for this book first came to me in the late spring of 1995 when I was eighteen years old and about to graduate from Central High School in Philadelphia. The manuscript was, for the most part, written and completed during my four years as a student at Penn State University from 1996 thru 1999. Following my graduation from college, I spent some months unsuccessfully trying to find a literary agent to assist me in publishing my manuscript. Ultimately, time constraints, primarily related to the start of my career in the business world, caused me to put aside my goal of publishing this story. The years passed. The manuscript sat.

In early 2007, my career having matured, I fully awakened to the widening debate in this country about issues related to the wars being waged in Iraq and Afghanistan. I reminded myself that the manuscript contained what I considered to be timely and critical messages on several of those matters. For that and other reasons, I concluded that the manuscript ought not continue gathering dust on a shelf. Now that my initial objective of publishing "Fishing With Hand Grenades" has been achieved, I hope that the story will not only inspire others as it has me, but that it will also have a positive impact on how we Americans, notwithstanding our political affiliations or personal views of our country's actions overseas, regard and treat our servicemen and women as they return home from serving our country in a war zone.

Ari Pontz
June 2008

Bibliography

The majority of the information in this book was obtained from interviews I conducted with "Danny Sullivan" during the summer of 1995. Unfortunately, memories do fade. In addition, it is often necessary to protect the identity of individuals. As a result, names of people and places may have been changed. Also, to preserve the style of the book, much of the context of the interviews was edited and/or paraphrased. These changes in no way affect the events that took place. If anything, I hope that they help to better express personal memories, emotions, and feelings.

All "Command Chronologies" and "After Action Reports" were obtained from the Marine Corps Historical Center, Washington Navy Yard, Washington, DC. The language drawn from those reports has not been edited.

All letters and journal entries in this book are fictional. They have been composed by the author based on actual events.

All the maps found at the beginning of this book were obtained from *The Battle for Khe Sanh*.

My sincerest gratitude to David Douglas Duncan, who graciously gave me his personal permission to include photographs he took during his eight days at Khe Sanh. His book *I Protest!* was at once striking, inspirational, and moving.

I would also like to make special reference to Eric Hammel's *Khe Sanh: Siege in the Clouds*, which greatly influenced the style and substance of this book.

Books

Dougan, Clark, Stephen Weiss and the editors of Boston Publishing Co.; *The American Experience in Vietnam*. New York: Norton; Boston: Boston Publishing Co., 1988.

Duncan, David Douglas, *I Protest!* New York: The New American Library, 1968.

Edelman, Bernard, edited for the New York Vietnam Veterans Memorial Commission, *Dear America: Letters Home From Vietnam*. New York: Norton, 1985.

Esper, George and the Associated Press, *The Eyewitness History of the Vietnam War, 1961-1975*. New York: Ballantine Books, 1983.

Hammel, Eric, *Khe Sanh: Siege in the Clouds*. New York: Crown Publishing, Inc., 1989.

Lopes, Sal & Michael Norman, *The Wall: Images and Offerings from the Vietnam Veterans Memorial*. San Francisco: Collins Pub, 1987.

Lung, Hoang Ngoc, *The General Offensives of 1968-69*. Washington, DC: US Army Center of Military History, 1981.

Nalty, Bernard C., *Air Power and the Fight for Khe Sanh*. Washington, DC: US Air Force, 1973.

Olson, James S., ed., *Dictionary of the Vietnam War*. New York: Greenwood Press, 1988.

Pearson, Willard, *The War in the Northern Provinces*. Washington, DC: Department of the Army, 1975.

Pisor, Robert, *The End of the Line: The Siege of Khe Sanh*. New York: WW Norton & Co. Inc., 1982.

Shore, Captain Moyers S., *The Battle for Khe Sanh.* Washington, DC: US Marine Corps, 1969.

Stanton, Shelby, *The Rise and Fall of an American Army: US Ground Forces in Vietnam, 1965-1973.* Novato, California: Presidio Press, 1985.

Warren, James A., *Portrait of a Tragedy: America and the Vietnam War.* New York: Lothrop, Lee & Shepard Books, 1990.

Westmoreland, William C., *A Soldier Reports.* New York: Dell Publishing, 1980.

Periodicals

"Battle Line-Up." *Time*, March 8, 1968, p. 19.

"Battle of Hue." *Time*, February 16, 1968, pp. 34-37.

"Fall of Lang Vei." *Time*, February 16, 1968, pp. 37-38.

"Fighting Pitch." *Time*, May 10, 1968, pp. 32-37.

"General's Biggest Battle, The." *Time*, February 16, 1968, pp. 19-20.

"General's Gamble, The." *Time*, February 9, 1968, pp. 22-33.

Harris, Stewart. "An Efficient Slaughter." *Time*, April 5, 1968, p. 36.

"How the Battle for Khe Sanh Was Won." *Time*, April 19, 1968, pp. 30-32.

"Khe Sanh: 6,000 Marines Dug in for Battle." *Life*, February 9, 1968, pp. 26-27.

"Living on Air: How Khe Sanh is Sustained." *Time*, March 1, 1968, p. 19.

"Mass Murder at Hue." *Time*, May 10, 1968, p. 37.

"On the Defensive." *Time*, March 1, 1968, pp. 18-19.

"Profile of the Infiltrators." *Time*, January 26, 1968, p. 31.

"Showdown at Khe Sanh." *Time*, February 2, 1968, pp. 25-26.

"Shrinking Sanctuary." *Time*, April 26, 1968, p. 28.

Sider, Don. "Khe Sanh: Ready to Fight." *Time*, February 16, 1968, pp. 38-39.

"Victory at Khe Sanh." *Time*, April 12, 1968, pp. 29-30.

End Notes

Chapter 2
1. American Experience, p. 114.
2. Ibid., p. 72;
   Eyewitness History, p. 99.

Chapter 4
1. American Experience, pp. 115-116.
2. Portrait of a Tragedy, p. 95.
3. American Experience, pp. 120-121.
4. Portrait of a Tragedy, p. 96.
5. Time, Feb 9, p. 32.
6. Life, Feb 9, p. 26.
7. Battle for Khe Sanh, pp. 6-7.
8. Ibid., pp. 10-17.
9. Ibid., p. 181.
10. Siege in the Clouds, p. 9.
11. Rise and Fall, p. 225.
12. End of the Line, p. 83.
13. Ibid.
14. Siege in the Clouds, p. 11.
15. End of the Line, p. 96
16. Battle for Khe Sanh, p. 27.

Chapter 5
1. Siege in the Clouds, p. 14.
2. Ibid., p. 16.
3. Ibid., p. 18.
4. Battle for Khe Sanh, p. 30.
5. End of the Line, p. 108.

Chapter 6
1. Time, Feb 2, p. 25.
2. Life, Feb 9, p. 26
3. Time, Feb 9, p. 31.
4. Life, Feb 9, p. 26.
5. Time, Feb 9, pp. 31-32.

6. Time, Feb 2, p. 25.
7. Ibid.
8. Rise and Fall, p. 249.
9. Time, Feb 2, p. 26.
10. Time, Feb 9, p. 22.
11. Rise and Fall, p. 231.
12. Ibid., p. 222.
13. Time, Feb 9, pp. 30-31.
14. Rise and Fall, p. 245.

Chapter 7
1. Time, March 1, p 19.
2. Time, Feb 16, p. 37;
Rise and Fall, p. 251.
3. Battle for Khe Sanh, pp. 121-122.
4. Time, March 1, p. 18.
5. Battle for Khe Sanh, p. 122.

Chapter 8
1. Time, April 19, p. 30.
2. Battle for Khe Sanh, p. 101.
3. Time, April 19, p. 31.
4. Air Power, p. 59;
Time, April 19, p. 30.

Chapter 10
1. Battle For Khe Sanh, p. 129;
1/26 Command Chronology, March 30, 1968, p. 8.
2. Battle for Khe Sanh, p. 130.
3. Ibid.
4. End of the Line, p. 259.
5. A Soldier Reports, p. 273.
6. Rise and Fall, p. 272.
7. End of the Line, p. 262.

Chapter 11
1. Siege in the Clouds, p. 415.
2. Life, April 19, 1968, p. 83;

Rise and Fall, p. 256;
Air Power, p. 60.
3. Time, April 12, p. 30.
4. Air Power, p. 112.
5. Time, April 12, p. 30.
6. Rise and Fall, p. 258.

Chapter 12
1. Time, April 26, p. 28.
2. Time, May 10, p. 32.
3. Time, April 26, p. 28.
4. Time, May 10, pp. 32-37.

Chapter 14
1. Battle for Khe Sanh, p.186.

Chapter 15
1. Time, May 10, p. 37.
2. Ibid.
3. Time, April 5, p. 36.
4. Time, Feb 9, p. 30.
5. Ibid., p. 22.
6. Time, April 5, p. 36;
Time, May 10, p. 37.
7. The Wall, p. 15.